Letters to Dead People

An entertaining look at the achievements of key
people in history

Ivor Share & Henry Nash

ISHN Publishing
Email: ishn_publishing@icloud.com

First Printing, 2022

ISBN: 978-1-7391832-0-2 (hardback)
ISBN: 978-1-7391832-2-6 (paperback)
ISBN: 978-1-7391832-1-9 (eBook)

For our respective partners, Denise and Susan, who travel with us through
our own span of history.

Contents

Forward...9
Introduction...11
The Letters..15
   Art & Literature................................17
      Letter to Sir Arthur Conan Doyle..........19
      Letter to Sappho..............................23
      Letter to William Shakespeare............25
      Letter to Josephine Baker..................27
      Letter to Beatrix Potter.....................29
      Letter to Walt Disney........................31
      Letter to Sir Christopher Wren............33
      Letter to Gerry Anderson..................35
      Letter to Chaucer.............................37
      Letter to Dick Rowe..........................40
      Letter to Johannes Gutenberg............42
      Letter to Lancelot Brown...................44
      Letter to Michelangelo......................46
      Letter to Samuel Pepys......................47
      Letter to Mark Twain.........................49
      Letter to Mar Saba...........................51
      Letter to Fred Astaire........................53
      Letter to James Halliwell-Phillipps........55
      Letter to Leonardo da Vinci................57
      Letter to Aristarchus of Samothrace.......58
      Letter to HG Wells............................60
      Letter to Enid Blyton.........................62
      Letter to Richard D'Oyly Carte...........64
      Letter to Charles Dickens...................67
      Letter to Theodor Seuss Geisel...........70
      Letter to Douglas Adams....................71
   Science, Engineering & Technology.............73
      Letter to Percy Shaw.........................75
      Letter to Rosalind Franklin.................77
      Letter to James Watt.........................79
      Letter to Edward Jenner.....................81

Letter to Alphonse Laveran 83
Letter to Samuel Morse 85
Letter to Joseph Priestley 88
Letter to Gustaf Dalén 91
Letter to Erwin Schrödinger 93
Letter to Neil Armstrong 94
Letter to William Durant 95
Letter to Henry Heimlich 97
Letter to Count Ferdinand von Zeppelin . 100
Letter to Percy Spencer 103
Letter to Archimedes 106
Letter to Carl Linnaeus 108
Letter to Alexander Graham Bell 110
Letter to HAL 113
Letter to Henry Ford 115
Letter to Raymond Davis 117
Letter to Orville Wright (1st attempt) 119
Letter to Orville Wright (2nd attempt) ... 121
Letter to Max Planck 123
Letter to Justus von Liebig 126
Letter to Amelia Earhart 128
Letter to Isaac Newton 130
Letter to Charles Darwin 133
Letter to Wilhelm Roentgen 135
Letter to Gottlieb Daimler 137
Letter to Emil von Wolff 139
Letter to Mary Anning 141
Letter to Glenn Curtiss 143
Letter to Werner Heisenberg 146
Letter to Marie Curie 148
Letter to Michael Faraday 149
Letter to Galileo Galilei 151
Retail & Commerce 153
Letter to Christopher Columbus 155
Letter to John Harvey Kellogg 158
Letter to Mary Brailsford 160
Letter to John Pemberton 162

Letter to Mary Fields 165
Letter to Marco Polo 167
Letter to Isaac Le Maire 169
Letter to Jack O'Neill 171
Letter to John Montagu 173
Letter to Robert McCulloch 175
Letter to William J. A. Bailey 178
Letter to Clarence Saunders 180
Letter to Orville Redenbacher 183
Letter to Milton Hershey 185
Letter to Henry Heinz 187
Letter to Elizabeth Magie 189
Letter to William Blackstone 191
Letter to Harland Sanders 193
Letter to Ray Kroc 196
Letter to Hanno the Navigator 198
Letter to Dom Perignon 201
Politics & Humanities 203
Letter to Boudica 205
Letter to Nettie Honeyball 207
Letter to Henry VIII 209
Letter to Jeremiah Dixon 211
Letter to Cai Lun 214
Letter to William Seward 216
Letter to Napoleon I, II and III 218
Letter to David Dyce Sombre 221
Letter to Sir Walter Raleigh 223
Letter to Confucius 225
Letter to Annie Taylor 227
Letter to James Ussher 228
Letter to Annie Londonderry 230
Letter to Queen Charlotte of Mecklenburg-Strlitz
                                            232
Letter to Florence Nightingale 234
Letter to King Arthur 236
Letter to Julius Caesar 238
Letter to The Grand Old Duke of York ...240

Letter to Albert Mansbridge 242
Letter to Aristotle 244
Letter to Nostradamus 247
Letter to Winston Churchill 248
Letter to Gertrude Ederle 250
Letter to Maximus' Lawyers 252
Epilogue 255
Letter to Steve Jobs 257
Acknowledgements 261
Citations 263

Forward

When the first batch of letters arrived in our office from Mr Timothy Shift, we had the same reaction we suspect you will have as you start reading this book. We assumed this was a prank that one of our friends was inflicting on us. However, having called our friends (that didn't take long) and becoming convinced they were innocent (at least of this charge), we were left none the wiser. Over the coming weeks and months, more letters arrived along with instructions to publish them together in a volume. The more we read them and started to look at the impact they appear to have made on history, the more we began to feel that perhaps we had misjudged them.

As you will see from the Introduction he provided, Mr Shift claims to have discovered a method of sending messages back in time. He has chosen to use letters for this back-in-time communication and has written a whole raft of them to people across the ages, some famous, some not so well known. You may recall that Donald Rumsfeld, the United States Secretary of Defence from 1975 - 1977, famously once coined the phrase, the "Unknown unknowns". Here, however, that phrase took on a whole new meaning. We didn't really know who Timothy was, where he was or even *when* he was. And that last point is a phrase you don't hear said very often! However, despite our initial misgivings, we felt the letters spoke for themselves, and hence, as per his request, we have collated those we have received into this book for publication.

Unfortunately, Mr Shift didn't provide any instructions on how to order or group these letters - so we have done the best we can. Nor do we have any indication if there are more on the way. Indeed, some may have gone astray and be missing from this collection. Inevitably, he will get to read this volume himself at some time, and let us know, no doubt by letter. If we do receive more, we will try to bring them to you in a further publication. Perhaps he will also provide some clarity about the mechanism he is using to get the letters to us and their original recipients - although there may be good reasons to keep this a secret.

As we read the letters, we often had to go and look up some of the references - which turned out to be more enjoyable than we had expected. We learnt, or were reminded of, many of the subtle twists in the evolution of science, technology, art, literature and politics - and we would encourage you to check them out too. We found this to be very rewarding and we hope you do as well.

Ivor & Henry
Curators & Editors of this first collection of letters
September 2022

Introduction

I'm writing this in 2046. Of course, you don't believe that, since you probably don't believe time travel exists. While the concept of time travel is commonplace in science fiction literature and film, most think that it is just that, fiction. However, you might have also heard it said that Einstein's theories don't actually prohibit time travel and believe me, he knew a thing or two about time and space. However, that just causes a lot of talk about what happens if you go back in time and kill off your own ancestors, then how could you still exist etc.?

However, the thing that most people have failed to focus on is that sending data back in time is a whole different ball game - and potentially a lot more interesting. In fact, that's my little secret - I've discovered how to send messages to people in the past. It took a while to perfect, and then once I had it working, I realised there was one final tricky part - that of ensuring the data is readable by the intended recipient. That really took me a while to get right, for example, you wouldn't want to send Henry VIII an email, would you?

For that reason, I decided the one and only medium that works across time, is a humble, old-fashioned, letter. Normally you write down what you want to say, put it in an envelope and stick a stamp on it. Currently that will cost you £52.46 (the Post Office, or Moonpig as they are now known, put the price up yet again in May 2044). Even at that price, despite being pretty good at random dates in the future, they can't cope with a targeted delivery date that is in the past. So, I used my messaging idea to send them for free. Back in time that is.

Well, lots of chat about the future, but little regarding what this book is all about. It's a collection of these letters I sent to famous people over the ages. All letters from me. Once I started, I found I couldn't stop! Want to know what these famous people said in return? Simple. Just read about them in either their own writings, general literature or other published historical accounts - it's all there. I'd like to think that these letters perhaps add the extra dimension to their own writings. Why did they say this? Why did they do that? It would be unpardonably arrogant to suggest I had any undue influence on their actions, but perhaps the astonishing notions some of the recipients seem to have had might be due to their thinking further along the lines I merely highlighted. Ironically, one the hardest things about this letter writing has been knowing exactly where to send them - historical records are somewhat vague as to where people were actually living. In some cases, I unfortunately ended up delivering letters to other people of the same name by mistake. I left some of these in here, just so you can see that I wasn't always successful.

Having written all these, and since I found the insights it gave me so interesting, I felt I wanted to share them, getting them published in some form. However, that brought up another problem. If I just used a book publisher in 2046, there would have been a whole hoo-ha and everyone would want to get in on the act, sending letters to their dead relatives when they were still alive. *"Papa, I love you. Where did you leave the $20million in Bearer Bonds? - Love Nicole"*. You get the picture. So, I thought if I used a publisher from the 2020s, they would be healthily sceptical, and might not delve so deeply. To this end, I managed to contact a couple of editors/collators (by letter of course) and I am getting them to collate all the letters into a book.

Now you may have spotted a potential flaw in my approach - and that is the concern I mentioned at the start of this Introduction about time travel, which is still valid even when sending letters. Therefore, I have to come clean and admit that my name isn't really Timothy Shift, that's a pseudonym. Once these letters are public, I really don't want someone tracking down my grandfather Alfred and bumping him off. That would end this jaunt pretty quick. If you get to read this, then you know that I'm safe (at least for now).

Well, normally, when starting out on a potential publishing venture like this, it is customary to hope for good luck. However, in this case I know it will be successful. I have already read the book.

Ad Praeteritum!

Timothy Shift
London, 2046

The Letters

Art & Literature

Targeted Delivery Date: 1892

Sir Arthur Ignatius Conan Doyle, KStJ, DL
Windlesham Manor
Crowborough
Sussex
England

Dear Sir Arthur,

I'll come straight to the point. I sincerely believe you can offer some assistance with a problem I have. I want to become a writer. Well not so much a writer per se, but I want to become known for the publication of my letters. My goal is to collate all my letters to famous people such as yourself. In fact, I'm delighted to tell you that you are my first correspondent. However, regarding my publishing goal, even though I have one great advantage, I still struggle with two distinct difficulties.

The first is that I am not, by nature, a particularly gifted writer. Gifted? I flatter myself. Proficient might have been the term I had hoped for but frankly, once you've read this letter, I believe we will both summarise my writing as, well, functional. I am hopeful however that, with practice, this will improve. To date, I am planning to circumvent this handicap, believing that interest in the fascinating lives and deeds of the recipients of my letters will carry the day. However, this makes plain problem number two.

These letters have not been written by the great and the good to whom they are addressed but unfortunately, they're all written by me. I still suspect my readers will really want to hear of the exploits, insights and foresights of these interesting people. Certainly, I can extol the virtues, convictions, astonishing deeds of my correspondents - or even perhaps highlight some quirky turn of event that has befallen them. For example, how you were once a medical doctor on board a whaling ship in the arctic. Or how you tried to set up your own private medical practice in Southsea, but because nobody turned up you spent your time learning how to write fiction instead. Perhaps that is where the ideas began to germinate for the future exploits of Mr Holmes and Dr Watson? Ultimately, of course, my letters are but biographical in nature, albeit with a degree of the inquisitorial thrown in for good measure. I am trying, therefore, to find an additional angle I could apply to make them even more interesting.

Those are my two problems - but I mentioned a unique advantage, one that brings to bear an incomparable range of questioning. What is the source of my peerless interrogative skills? 20:20 hindsight, that's what! You see I am from the future, and I am sending you this letter through the only medium with which I can communicate back through the years.

Naturally, I first need to establish my credentials with you that I am truly from the future. I'm not going to wax on about upcoming world affairs or financial stocks from which you could profit, as such measures are strictly beyond my remit. I'll restrict myself to a simple fact about which only you (and I) could know the future outcome. Next year, you are going to publish another Holmes novel called "The Final Problem", in which Professor Moriaty and Sherlock Holmes, both plunge to their deaths over the Richenbach Falls in Meiringen in Germany.

I really don't know if you have yet thought of arranging that particular finale for your famous sleuth, let alone committed yourself to publishing such an outcome? Therefore, this letter gives rise to two possible scenarios. The first is that I have directly influenced the plot line of a famous Sherlock Holmes novel. If that is the case, then I am honoured and thankful in equal measure since you will have helped address my first problem, that of becoming a writer. Irrespective, most people will believe you are the sole author of this story. If you were to claim otherwise, with your reputation on certain matters of spiritualism, people will just contend that

Arthur Conan Doyle is hearing those voices again. Alternatively, perhaps you already have that ending in mind and it may be that you do not believe my claims. If your scepticism prevails, all I ask at this juncture is for you to keep this letter safe and refer back to it at some stage in the future. Indeed, perhaps you might give it a name, such as a *prophecy of the future?* However, regarding the story itself, one thing I might suggest is that you consider giving yourself "an out" which would enable you to bring Mr Homes back, should you so desire. You may not realise it, but unlike the deaths of other fictional characters, the public have taken to your characters so strongly that there will be a public outcry upon you bumping him off. Maybe you could just *imply* that he is dead, perhaps with nobody actually witnessing the event - thus leaving the opportunity for his return at a later date? Hmm, maybe I am becoming a writer after all. I am also seeing a potential solution to my second problem, that of providing the odd hint that might result in a minor change in future direction.

Finally, I have some more information for you, the underlying current of which will delight you no end. I realise that in 1892 giving the residence of Sherlock Holmes as 221B Baker Street seemed safe enough (since the numbers only went up to 84 in the nineteenth century). However, I have to tell you that following expansion of the street, the current occupants of 220-222 Baker Street are fed up to their back teeth with tourists flocking there with selfie-sticks, blocking the doors etc. Sherlock Holmes aficionados seeking Sherlock's Homes, you might say. A bank that owned the building had to hire a full-time secretary purely to respond to the mail sent to Mr Holmes at this address, as sadly Mrs Hudson's relatives are nowhere to be found.

I will try to write to you again. I am aware of your interests, and I need to find a way to convince you that my letters are wholly based on hard science and in no way are associated with psychic phenomena or spiritualism. Oh yes, and we really need to have a serious talk about your well-published endorsement of photographs of some fairies at the bottom of the garden.

It seems you are indeed helping me as it's elementary, my dear Conan Doyle. You see, I have <u>time</u> on my side!

Yours sincerely,

Timothy Shift*

p.s What's a selfie-stick? Hmm, maybe I'll leave that to another letter.

---

* Editors' note: As this appears to be the first letter Mr Shift wrote, it seemed right that this should be the first one in our collection. Readers might well notice how, in subsequent letters, he develops his techniques along the lines outlined here.

Targeted Delivery Date: 598 BC

Sappho
℅ The family Cleïs
Lesbos
Ancient Greece

Dear Sappho,

I must admit, it is a bit daunting to know how to write to, or even address, a poet as renowned as yourself. You have been called *The Poetess*, in the same way that Homer is often called *The Poet*. Although we know you were prolific in your written works by reputation from references in other texts of the time, very little of your actual verse has survived. Estimates are that you may have written around 10,000 lines of poetry, of which sadly only around 650 lines have been discovered so far. In fact, we only have one poem of yours that is considered complete, "Ode to Aphrodite".

This letter, I realise, reaches you at a difficult time, since you have been exiled. Although there is some confusion as to your whereabouts (some people favour you may have gone to Sicily), I am betting you have returned to your family home on Lesbos, and hopefully you can continue writing. I also realise that, in your time, your descriptions of the love between women were not considered particularly scandalous, rather people appreciated the tenderness and beauty of your writing. Sadly that hasn't always been the case, and for centuries after you, authors, playwrights, and so called experts (who were invariably men) have tried to cast you as some kind of tragic promiscuous heterosexual (even suggesting you will throw yourself off a cliff due to your love of the local ferryman). Really sorry about all that, but times change you know. Today, I'm delighted to say society is perhaps more in tune with your own ideas and people can (more or less) profess their love regardless of their gender. In many countries, I am pleased to tell you, that you can even marry who you love, again regardless of gender. Not everywhere, but we are getting there. In fact, because of where you grew up and the subject of many of your poems, you have had a direct impact on our modern language, with the term Lesbian being derived from your home island. I'd love to be able to report that modern tourism sees the Greek islands mainly as a sanctuary for love, and visits from the LGBT+ community. However, while they are indeed known for that in certain areas, they are also infamous for somewhat outrageous stag and hen dos, where twerking lessons are mandatory and inflatable versions of various body parts are held aloft as if in some modern ritual. Oh well, you can't get everything right I guess.

Regarding that fact that only a small portion of your work has survived, luckily we continue to discover small new fragments of your poems at a reasonable frequency. Only a few years ago some fragments were discovered in an ancient rubbish dump. I suspect that may concern and delight you - concern that your poems were assigned to the trash but pleased that we are still looking for, and managing to find, new pieces. I fear for what will happen when people a few millennia in my future decide to dig up our current rubbish dumps. What will they make of what they find? One would hope that, as with your works, we'd be remembered for the grace of our writing. The purity of our thoughts and arguments. The wisdom of our poets. Instead, will they just wonder who the hell bought all those "Pet Rocks", "Tickle Me Elmos", and funny looking cubes that had 9 different colour stickers on each of their sides? I shudder to think what they will make of us.

Keep up the writing, it will be appreciated more than you know.

Yours sincerely,

Timothy Shift

Targeted Delivery Date: 23 June 1613

William Shaxberd/Shappere/Shakespeare
Stratford-upon-Avon
Warwickshire
England

Dear Will,

I wanted to write again to thank you for taking such swift action based upon my recommendations in my previous letter. I can confirm that whatever you did with the script of your Cardenio play (surreptitiously slipped it into the nearest chamber pot?), it has not been discovered - and it is now generally known as your "lost work". In addition, fair play in getting all the King's Men troupe to swear secrecy, so that no details of their performance of the play has been handed down.

I hope you can appreciate that my suggestion to destroy it was not based on a dislike of your work - in fact, the opposite is true. I just felt that writing Cardenio as your big "reveal" play in the way you did, would have affected the views of so many people regarding some of your most loved characters. For example:

- The fact that Romeo and Juliet was not, after all, based on the characters from *The Tragicall Historye of Romeus and Juliet* by Arthur Brooke, but instead was based on a tryst between Basil & Eustice who pull pints at The George and the Leg of Mutton Inns respectively; all set against the backdrop of a long running argument as to which public house sold the best pork scratchings. This might have severely dented what people read into that play.

- Your revelation that MacBeth wasn't actually Scottish, but was actually a sanctimonious winkle seller on the banks of the

Thames, would have made a laughing stock of all those actors whispering that they were in "the Scottish play" to avoid the bad luck of calling it by its real name. Further, it would have been cold comfort that he was nicknamed MacBeth because he once sold a dodgy basket of eels to a scruffy bloke in a kilt.

- The fact that you reveal the typo in the manuscript for A Merchant of Venice, that Shylock actually demands a *pound of fish* since he is short of protein for supper, would have just invalidated so many famous uses of this misquoted phrase.

- You would be shocked at the time and effort historians have spent trying to uncover what you were doing in the years 1585-1592. Baseless theories abound, from schoolteacher, to shipping clerk, to poacher-on-the-run. The fact, as you revealed in the play, that you were actually a copy writer for The Marlowe Publishing Company would have really got the tongues wagging.

Finally, the rumours that you and your friends planted, that Cardenio was in fact based on an adventure of Don Quixote, have spread exceedingly well. This is now the view held by scholars, hence covering up the above. Nicely done - a plot worthy of a bard of the finest order!

Yours sincerely,

Timothy Shift

p.s. I hope you like the fact that I slipped into this letter 5 words or phrases that you actually invented ;-)

p.p.s. What does the ;-) symbol mean? Try turning the letter sideways. It's part of a trend that is the very antithesis of all you stand for with your love of the English language. I think you would loathe it.

Targeted Delivery Date: August 1961

Josephine Baker
Château des Milandes
Castelnaud-la-Chapelle
Dordogne
France

Dear Josephine,

Congratulations on recently receiving the French Croix de Guerre, the Médaille de la Résistance, and the Légion d'Honneur, for your work during World War II with the resistance and the Deuxième Bureau (French military intelligence agency). Probably not what you had expected growing up, sometimes living rough, in St. Louis, Missouri in the early 1900s, when opportunities must have looked thin on the ground. Despite all the success you had as a dancer and singer (even becoming the most successful American entertainer in France), it is these honours, along with having adopted twelve children and your fight against racial segregation, that really speak to me as to your true self.

It's funny how people you meet can change your life - with you getting to know "Bricktop" (so called for her red hair and freckles) after moving to Paris, France all those years ago in the 1920s. She was probably the only other lady of colour in the industry there - and I'm sure you supported each other. I have always wondered what gave you the idea for your famous "banana dress" you used in the *danse sauvage*. Whatever it was, it went down a storm. What sets it apart, however, is how you didn't play to the stereotype - which just made it more popular! You became a sensation! Today, I'm not sure someone could pull that off - we have enough trouble with racist idiots throwing bananas onto football pitches thinking they are being clever. Despite your forcefulness insisting on not playing to segregated audiences (especially when touring the USA), we still have a way to go on this score. It is America's loss that the slow progress in their civil rights movement means that your visits there are few - your continued and increasing involvement in the movement is a credit to you. My advice is to ignore any nay-sayers and grab whatever opportunities come your way to use your status to push the agenda forward, although I appreciate family comes first. You have never been afraid to "open your big mouth" and speak out, and your life struggle against segregation would resonate in any speech you give. Hopefully you and Dr Martin Luther King will get a chance to meet and compare your dreams for the future.

Closer to home, despite you feigning shock every time it happens during a show, I'm pretty sure you secretly trained *Chiquita* (your pet Cheetah) to leap into the orchestra pit and terrorise those assembled. The audiences loved it, even if it did decrease the life-expectancy of jazz musicians of the era. It's a tough business you are in, as you have experienced, and I think perhaps you feel that the fire burning inside you is lower than it was before. However, I think you will find that even the embers of Josephine Baker are enough to set light to many a stage or audience.

Good luck for the future.

Yours sincerely,

Timothy Shift

Targeted Delivery Date: September 1912

Beatrix Potter
℅ Hilltop Farm
Sawrey
The Lake District
England

Dear Beatrix,

I wanted to send my congratulations on your engagement to William Heelis. Hopefully you can now put the past behind you, and the sad death of your previous fiancé, some 7 years ago. Your writings have continued apace, however, throughout this time, with books such as *The Tale of Jemima Puddle-Duck* following up the success of *The Tale of Peter Rabbit*. I wonder if you think back and still remember all those rejections to Peter (or "the bunny book" as it was called) when you first tried to get it published? Such were the problems that you had 200 copies printed yourself for your friends and family. Perseverance, is indeed, a virtue. I am also impressed with the fact that you have worked hard on the merchandising, with Peter Rabbit dolls etc. You really are ahead of almost everyone on this - and, if you have time, perhaps you could drop a line to a young animator by the name of Walt Disney, currently in Kansas City, and explain how this works.

I did want to comment, however, on the first in a rumoured new range of books that you are planning, aimed at adults. I have only seen an early draft, but some of the scenes are quite haunting. One in particular concerns me - when the spurned mistress of Mr McGregor breaks back into his house and boils a rabbit in a pot on the cooker. Surely not Flopsy, Mopsy or Cotten-tail? Or worse, Peter? Your draft doesn't say - but the implication is there - and it is pretty disturbing, reflecting perhaps the fatal attraction we have to this darker side. I appreciate your desire to branch out into other genres, but maybe this is a step too far? It's a side of you we have not seen before, and it's frightening - I fear for your audience. There would be no shame in shelving the project, and in any case, good ideas like this tend to resurface anyway.

Yours sincerely,

Timothy Shift

Targeted Delivery Date: February 1927

Walt Disney, % The Walt Disney Studio
Burbank
California, United States of America

Dear Walt,

I am delighted to be able to write to you and get the chance to speak to such an up-and-coming animator. Your ideas and plans to revolutionise animated films are truly ground-breaking, and I predict great things.

I know that your ideas for the subject matter of your films are still being developed, so I just wanted to throw my two cents' worth into the pot as to what might or might not work. It seems you are intending for all your productions to be in the gothic horror genre. Although I agree this is popular, I wonder if you might consider a change of tack, since I am unsure we are ready for animated versions of this type? Some of my concerns/suggestions are as follows:

- Your planned production called *Chainsaw Willy*, about a blood thirsty rodent attempting to pass himself off as senior officer in order to find his prey is quite unique, but I am unsure it will play well to the demographics. Perhaps you could rework it with a nautical theme and a more benevolent main character?

- I believe you are working on a state-of-the-art feature film, with a current working title of *The Dark Dominatrix and the Seven Zombies*. I know this is pushing the current capabilities of animation - and many in the industry think it may bankrupt you before you can complete it. They are calling it "Disney's Folly"! I admire your determination to prove them wrong, I really do. Here's an idea - confuse the hell out of them by turning the tables and flipping the content. I don't know, make it something pristine and pure, with maybe cheerful chappies (e.g. along the lines of chimney sweeps, gnomes or similar?) instead of zombies. You have plenty of creative types there, I am sure they can come up with something. Get this right, and it could be the making of the company.

- Further out, I think you are planning to move into more live action films, maybe with some blended animation. Sounds like a great idea. If I understand it correctly, I think the working title is *Carrie the Nanny comes from the sky*? First, I'm not sure if Carrie sounds like scary horror character, but I could be wrong. I think the plot involves kidnapping children via a siren's call, along with bewitching the head of the house to accept investing in blood sucking avians. I have to say it sounds pretty far out. I would advise against focusing on the avians - who ever heard of a horror film where birds are the stars?! My suggestion would be to instead hide a darker back story about a woman whose father dies of alcoholism and can't face the sight of blood (or anything red) within a nice fluffy tale of teaching children (and particularly their parents) how to enjoy life. You could still keep with the Nanny theme if you insist. Oh, and if those chimney sweeps aren't right to replace the seven zombies, you could always throw a few of them into this one.

I look forward to seeing how these turn out - and I hope I haven't upset your plans too much with the above suggestions.

All the best,

Timothy Shift

p.s. You may have received a letter from a lady in England by the name of Beatrix Potter - hopefully her ideas on merchandising were of help.

Targeted Delivery Date: January 1723

Sir Christopher Wren
St James Street
Mayfair
London
England

Sir,

I really don't know where to start with this letter. My office floor is, metaphorically speaking, strewn with torn up copies.

It started when I was asked to write to you regarding a disturbing accusation with respect to your architecture. The truth is I had absolutely no idea how prolific you have been. Not only have you been one of the most highly acclaimed English architects in history, but your reputation is also outstanding as an anatomist, astronomer, geometer, and mathematician-physicist.

I understand you were given responsibility for rebuilding more than fifty churches in the City of London after the Great Fire in 1666. This included St Paul's Cathedral on Ludgate Hill, which was completed in 1710, and is today generally regarded as your masterpiece. That's before considering other notable buildings by you including the Old Royal Naval College, Greenwich, the Royal Hospital Chelsea, and parts of Hampton Court Palace.

Your education in Latin and Aristotelian physics, at the University of Oxford, along with the foundation of the Royal Society (in which you served as president from 1680 to 1682), made your scientific work highly regarded by many eminent scientists of your era (for example Blaise Pascal and Isaac Newton). This work alone would have you in the annals of the greats. But you are an ambitious chap and, quite reasonably, you wanted more.

I'm not entirely sure when you started thinking about the new design for St Paul's Cathedral. Maybe you got inspiration from your trip to Paris in 1665. A trip to study the architecture and to peruse the drawings of Bernini, the great Italian sculptor and architect, who himself was visiting Paris at the time. In any case, after returning from Paris, you made your first drafts for St Paul's.

You tried to get King Charles II to agree to your new plans for the city well before the fire, but he didn't really see the need. You must have been gutted (pun intended) when he rejected them. So rather convenient wasn't it, that barely a week after you get back from France, plans for the new buildings across London under your arm, the Great Fire of London mysteriously comes along and destroys two-thirds of the city. A little suspicious if I may say. Motive. Opportunity. I'm not expecting to find a smoking gun. More likely a smoking oven in the bakers in Pudding Lane. Nonetheless, here you are, having been appointed as King's Surveyor of Works in 1669, so you clearly had a hand in rebuilding the city after all.

Look, I'm not acting in any official capacity, and I don't want to cast any aspersions about you - which is why I'm writing and suggesting you put your side of the story. I appreciate it's all very circumstantial. Of course, you may well choose to ignore this letter and history will have to draw its own conclusions.

Yours sincerely,

Timothy Shift

Targeted Delivery Date: March 1966

Gerry Anderson
% AP Films
Slough Trading Estate
Slough
United Kingdom

Dear Gerry,

Congratulations on the release of your latest TV series *Thunderbirds*, filmed in *Supermarionation* (so named since it is blend of the words *super*, *marionette* and *animation*). Getting the lip-syncing working with that solenoid embedded in the puppet must have been pretty challenging (along with all the various experiments in wire colour/thickness to try and hide them as best you could). Clever, also, how the subtle shooting angles & cutting (e.g. filming waist up whenever possible when they had to walk) got round the limitations in dexterity. I gather it was the real-life rescue of miners from the collapse in a German colliery in 1963 (known as the miracle of Lengede or "Wonder von Lengede") that inspired you to come up with the idea of International Rescue. In fact, I can let you into a secret that there is today a real organisation called International Rescue Corps, which helps out in times of disasters, that was inspired by your creation. Sadly, as far as I can tell, they have no permanent facilities on a Pacific island.

I know that series 2 of Thunderbirds has just been commissioned, and in addition you already have ideas on a totally new series with the working title of "Captain Pink and the Mystery of Eons" - sounds intriguing. With a bit of tweaking, I think the Americans should love this. I have no doubt that someone with your imagination has numerous other ideas/plans running round your brain. I have seen drafts of your early notes, but I think some of these may need revising, for example:

- Joe at 90: The story of a grandfather who is given special powers by his son, using implants in his dentures and zimmer frame.
- Lady Penelope does Dallas: Good luck with ensuring the puppeteers don't get their wires crossed on that one.
- Parker's Revenge: The story of a car that comes to life, with a red heartbeat on the grill and strange monotonous voice.
- Richard Wrench: The story of an animatronic spanner that has to investigate the mysterious goings at a bowling alley where all the balls have turned into parrots.

One other thought - I am sure you are watching the emerging NASA missions with awe. It strikes me that the moon would make a good base if the earth needed to defend itself against aliens, right? On that vein, did you read the article that said that prolonged exposure to low gravity can cause hair to turn a shade of purple, especially in women? I think it was published last year, at the beginning of April.

Finally, I'm sure you would be the first to recognise the help that Lew Grade has given AP Films, both in finance and support for your projects. Lew is thinking of working with an American puppeteer called Jim Henson (you may have heard of him). I am sure the two of you would have a lot in common - maybe try and get him to make an introduction? Even if it takes a while, you never know, there might be a chance of a project together, should time allow.

Yours sincerely,

Timothy Shift

Targeted Delivery Date: August 1392

Geoffrey Chaucer
Clerk of the Kings Works & Keeper of the Lodge
Feckenham Forest
Worcestershire
England

Dear Geoffrey,

I hope you don't mind me writing to you in Modern English, which I admit is somewhat different to the Middle English that you have made popular. You will notice that many of my words look similar, but some of the endings are different (in general, the trailing -e has gone, in most cases). Our pronunciations would be very different too - since there is a change afoot for you starting in a few years called *The Great Vowel Shift*. The good news is that this will provide a much greater standardisation of English. The bad news is that it creates the bane of many a school pupil's English literature course, trying to understand much of what you wrote!

Take your seminal work, *The Canterbury Tales*. Look, I know that many of the tales were re-works of earlier stories, but the framing - wow, that is novel! Nobody has ever created such a distinctive framing arc as a pilgrim group travelling to Canterbury to visit the shrine of Thomas Becket, and embedded the stories within it. Pure genius. Now, I am sure you have planned this whole project thoroughly, but I would make a few points if I may:

- According to your General Prologue, there are 29 pilgrims and I believe you want to record 4 tales from each (2 on the way to the shrine, 2 on the way back). Hopefully you don't need me to do the maths - but that's 116 tales. I know you are a busy man what with being the Clerk of the Kings Works (including the repairs that you have to organise to the *various* royal palaces and all), and

I think you have been squeezing the writing in for about five years now - so far you've only finished around 25 tales? And only the Nun has had a 2nd tale, let alone anyone having 4. Have you really thought this through? Not wishing to state the obvious, but given you are already in your 50s, you may need to wake up and smell the coffee (Hmm, given the date, maybe try malted grains?). Am I right in thinking that your main scrivener is one Adam Pinkhurst? If so, maybe he can hurry things up a bit making faster copies from your working draft?

- You are writing your tales in the London dialect of Middle English, and although this can be a cause of even more confusion, you may be pleased to know that confounding people using dialects is a tradition that hasn't been lost. Many a puzzled tourist to London Town has been told their hotel room is up the Apple & Pears, to give reception a call on the Dog & Bone should they need anything, and that they need to cough up a Monkey in terms of Bees & Honey to settle their Jack & Jill. Let's just say it separates the true travellers from the grockles - something that I am sure will resonate with you.

- While I am all for the ethos that it is the taking part that really counts, rather than who wins...I do wonder if the prize of a leg of mutton of somewhat dubious freshness and a couple of pints of ale at the Tabard Inn at Southwark will attract the calibre of story tellers you are seeking? Maybe throw in a couple of tickets for the winner (along with their significant other), chosen via public vote-off, to the Tower of London as well, now that you have finished the new wharf and tournament stands?

- The Miller's tale certainly causes a reasonable amount of shock and surprise at what goes on! I'd be surprised if people didn't turn white when hearing it - well, perhaps a whiter shade of pale, at least.

- Far be it from me to proffer any lines that might be worthy of inclusion in what will become your magnum opus, so I have lifted (and tweaked) a few lines from a modern dialect-driven poet, Pam Ayres:

> *A traveller gave me a friendship cake,*
> *I'd never met the fella,*
> *We served it up along the way,*
> *And all got salmonella*

As an aside, on a different topic, I bring heartfelt thanks from florists and insincere card manufactures throughout the modern world - due to the fact that you are the first person to write about the association between love and St. Valentine's Day, in your Parliament of Foules in 1382. Cupid has struck!

Anyway, best of luck in finishing your tales.

Yours sincerely,

Timothy Shift

Targeted Delivery Date: 2 January 1962

Dick Rowe, % Decca Records
London
United Kingdom

Dear Mr Rowe,

I gather that yesterday you had four lads from Liverpool (John Lennon, Paul McCartney, George Harrison & Pete Best, who are calling themselves *The Beatles*) in for an audition. This was after your colleague Mike Smith had gone to one of their Cavern Club performances in December. I am not sure of your view on how well it went, but it didn't seem to have gone too bad to me. I know that Mike was late to the audition due to celebrating a little too much the night before (well, it was New Year's Eve, and if you can't celebrate like it's your birthday on a day like that, when can you!).

Now and then you come across a band that really dig it. Don't ask me why I think these four have what it takes, it's on the tip of my tongue - maybe it's due to the fact that they have been friends for quite a while. That means a lot. They have built something that is different, after leaving home and relentlessly playing on tour, come rain or shine. I know what goes on when on the road, stays on the road (since one is free as a bird, and might do something daft like wear a toilet seat around your neck), but I guess that it is better than a road to nowhere. Man, it will be important that they get back in the studio to record their own self-compositions.

As you know only too well, the path to success for a new band is a long and winding road. A day in the life of a modern group has changed so much. You can say goodbye to all that stuffy, rigid approach to music - and any record label has to help and support the use of the emerging recording technology, that will enable a new revolution in music.

If you are indeed unsure about the band, I guess there is an outside chance that you and Brian Epstein can still work it out, and then it won't be long until we hear their music more widely. In my view, because they are so good, it wouldn't take any time at all until you would recoup your investment.

Wait, I know that you are under pressure to recommend only one act, between *The Beatles* and *Brian Poole and the Tremeloes*, with the latter haviing the advantage of being a local band (so you can more easily keep tabs on them). Nobody I know would like to have to carry that weight and make that decision! What I will say is that I don't really think that guitar bands have had their day (whatever people are telling you around the office).

If you do decide to turn them down, maybe you could tell me why, if and when you write your autobiography. Whatever happens, I am sure it won't be the end for them. In any case, tomorrow never knows, and there are some other great bands out there who you might want to look at, e.g. The Moody Blues, The Animals, Small Faces, Procol Harum and The Rolling Stones (ask George about them, I think he likes them). It is always important in life to look to the future, and as for the past, just let it be.

Yours sincerely,

Timothy Shift*

p.s. How did you find Pete's drumming - any problems with timing? If so, not exactly a ring(o) of confidence, I know.

---

* Editors' note: At first, we didn't quite understand all the contents of this letter, until we realised that Mr Shift had used it to slip numerous Beatles song titles into the text - 33 of them that we can spot!

Targeted Delivery Date: August 1448

Johannes Guttenberg
Mainz
Electorate of Mainz
Holy Roman Empire

Mein Lieber Johannes,

I was sorry to hear about the demise of your mirror-capture business - an interesting idea of using highly polished mirrors to capture holy images of religious relics, that you could then sell to pilgrims. I admire the entrepreneurial spirit! Cash flow can be a real killer when something like flooding delays the launch for a whole year - and I have to tell you that these kinds of events are only going to become more common. Although I'm not quite sure the tech you were using would really have worked - actually you were on the right lines. Although I can't speak to the religious value, today we can capture images like this in a thing called a Hologram. It's a bit hard to explain, but the results are remarkable.

I don't raise the above in order to criticise your business skills in any way - rather to ensure you are not discouraged. If I have got the timing of this letter right, you are now working on your next project - that of creating a mechanism to mass produce copies of documents and books - now known as "printing". I believe you plan to try this out on the holy book itself and enable the mass printing of the Bible. Nothing like taking on the big one to start! I really wouldn't worry about the grief and protests you are getting from the NUM (National Union of Monks). It will be illuminating to find out just how up in arms they will be. Anyway, that is to say, regarding you depriving them of their means of earning a crust - we all need to move with the times and hand copying has had its day!

You will be pleased to hear that printing really will transform almost everything including education, the arts, politics and literature. It enables the wide distribution of the absolute classics including the Works of Shakespeare, the romantic poets like Keats, science fiction from the likes of Isaac Asimov, 50 Shades of Grey, The Beano etc. All the greats. Unfortunately, this only makes up a small percentage of everything printed, while 99% of it is absolute drivel, and isn't worth the metal it was type-set with. Not your fault at all, there's no accounting for taste. In fact, it has now got worse than that. I'm not sure how big the first prototype is of your new machine? Now imagine if you could shrink it down and make it so cheap that everybody could own one. Furthermore, rather than the paper coming out of their personal machine, they might specify that work to emerge on any other machine around the world! Today we call this the "World Wide Web". You might call it unmitigated anarchy, and you would not be far wrong.

Anyway, good luck with the first machine - who knows where this might take us.

All the best,

Timothy Shift

p.s. What's "science fiction"? Oh, that's when people write about what might happen in the future, and invariably (if they are good at it) it does eventually come to pass. In fact, you just read some, but then I kind of cheated.

p.p.s. This letter is in a proportional justified font. Good luck with that.

Targeted Delivery Date: March 1741

Lancelot ("Capability") Brown
The Gardens at Stowe
Buckinghamshire
England

Dear Lancelot,

First of all, I hope this letter reaches you successfully, since my first attempt went to a 12th century knight who I doubt would have understood much of what I was talking about!

Congratulations on being made head gardener at Stowe, with the princely annual salary of £25 - you must be cock-a-hoop! It is a real step up in your career at the age of just 24.

I am sure you are starting to plan out your ideas, so I thought this might be a good time to review the results of your earlier commission for Mrs Ethel Jones, of Lillingstone Lovell, Buckinghamshire. I know Ethel was overjoyed with your transformation of the back garden of her one-up, one-down terraced house. In particular, she loved the group of garden gnomes, the one-hole crazy golf feature (with miniature windmill), the water bath made out of a recycled bedpan, and not forgetting the George II styled bird feeder. Fantastic work!

As well as that earlier commission went, I do wonder if perhaps you might need to revise your plans as you look at more ambitious projects in your new job, for example:

- For one, I just don't think the gnomes idea will scale up. You would need thousands of them at Stowe to create the same effect - the supply chain for producing that many would be a nightmare. I know the little darlings look kinda cute (especially the fellow with the fishing rod), but I'd recommend you look for something else. Perhaps use small clumps of trees in a group? At a distance they could have the same effect as groups of gnomes.

- While the sustainability credentials for recycling domestic items for water features is high, maybe you could take this a step further in scale and just "go back to nature"? Perhaps just try natural streams leading to lakes, get rid of all that formality, and see how it works out?

- The crazy-golf idea was good for entertainment - but how about also taking the miniaturisation-centric approach a bit further. Your clientele, in their large fancy houses, would love the idea of miniaturised versions of houses/chapels/temples etc. - you could squeeze one into a corner where the scale is hard to judge. Sounds a bit of a folly, I know, but you could give it a go.

- However, those bird feeders that allow the seeds to be eaten out of the mouth, nose and ears of George II are great - you should stick those everywhere, at least one every 30 yards or so.

I hope you don't mind the above suggestions - feel free to ignore any that you don't think will work out. I know how you like to describe a garden as having the "capability" to improve - that's a nice mantra, and you never know, as a nickname that might stick.

Yours sincerely,

Timothy Shift

Targeted Deliver Date: September 1503

Michelangelo di Lodovico Buonarroti Simoni
Caprese
Valtiberina, Near Arezzo
Tuscany

Dear Michelangelo,

I understand that the Overseers of the Office of Works of Florence Cathedral (who are members of the woollen cloth guild, known as the *Arte della Lana*), have commissioned a series of twelve large Old Testament sculptures for the buttresses of the cathedral. I also understand that Donatello has created a figure of Joshua in terracotta and that Agostino di Duccio has created a figure of Hercules, also in terracotta.

I would like to propose, if you can get a large block of Carrara marble, that a super-sized statue situated near the Pallazo della Signoria would be great. The subject is clearly your decision.

Just to get your creative juices flowing I wanted to make a small suggestion. I enclose a photo of myself in an appropriate pose. It's your call but if you think the form of my body might look good carved in marble, please do feel free to use these pictures for your initial sketches.

I certainly wouldn't want you to attribute it as being me. That would be quite inappropriate. However, a small acknowledgement, unidentifiable of course, would be great. My middle name is David. I never use it so that would be our little secret.

Hope that helps.

Timothy Shift

Targeted Delivery Date: October 1671

Samuel Pepys
The Navy Office Buildings, Seething Lane, Tower Hill
London
England

Dear Samuel,

My, you have been busy! Maybe everyone keeps regular diaries in your time, but you seem to be particularly prolific. Perhaps other people's diaries simply got lost, because in my time, yours stands out as the most detailed account we have of events in the middle of the 17th century. Starting in 1660 you have meticulously recorded anything and everything that you have witnessed. And I mean everything - wars, fires, plagues, life in parliament, your sexual exploits, what you had for breakfast, the various stages of gout in your friends, the extraction of your bladder stones, to name just a few. All the crucial events of the time! It is a good thing you left us a guide to enable us to translate your rather unique shorthand (with its mixture of French and other Mediterranean countries' words just to throw people off the scent), otherwise we might never have been able to read it.

I admire your calmness under pressure - for instance being able to nip back and have a full and satisfying dinner (with wine) while the Great Fire of London raged all around. As the flames closed in, you still found time not only to evacuate your wife (along with your savings), but also time to bury some of your finest wines, along with some excellent parmesan cheese. These days we just whack a whole camembert in the oven to melt it, but I do like your idea of using natural resources to provide a welcoming warm cheese and wine party. You don't speculate as to the cause of the fire - but personally, I think that chap Wren has questions to answer, arriving on the scene with ready made plans for a new look for London. I've written to him to express my suspicions - if you see him, you might like to ask him yourself (or at least ask that he gives me a hint of his guilt or innocence).

Another huge event you record in your diaries is, of course, the Great Plague of London in 1665-1666. You witnessed the terrible scenes of official recorded weekly deaths of nearly 7,000 (with unofficial estimates over 10,000/week), people ignoring curfews, and quack remedies being peddled left, right and centre (e.g. bottles of "plague-water" containing herbs). It has been estimated that a quarter of London's population perished. I am sure you are hoping that your great city would never again be caught so unprepared for such an event. I'm sorry to tell you that history has a way of repeating itself.

To be honest, I am slightly worried about some of the entries you have made in the last year and a half. Making comments about the King's relations with the likes of Nell Gwyn ("pretty, witty Nell" as you call her) can seriously get a man into trouble. Look what happened to the Member of Parliament Sir John Coventry - he made similar accusations and was attacked after he left the chamber and had his nose cut off. This has caused parliament to pass the Coventry Act (also known as the Maiming Act) to make such attacks on people such as Members of Parliament punishable by death. Sounds like a variant of the expression "to cut off your nose to spite your face"? Despite the passing of this act, I'd urge caution. If you do feel worried, how about you close down your diary writing for a bit? In fact, you could also hide away the last year or two's chapters, and make the diary finish, say, at the end of 1669, and avoid these comments coming to light? I gather you are increasingly worried about your health, so you could claim concern over your eyesight, or something like that?

Yours sincerely,

Timothy Shift

Targeted Deliver Date: 18th December 1908

Mark Twain
% Samuel Langhorne Clemens
Stormfield
Redding
Connecticut
United States of America

Dear Mr Clemens,

I am greatly relieved to learn that the reports of your death were merely "an exaggeration". I was a tad concerned I might find you <u>half</u> dead, the clarification being that you were not completely dead.

Forgive my seeming preoccupation with your ultimate demise. That is not my intention, so let me explain my problem. I am from the future, writing letters to those who have predeceased me. Writing letters to dead people is not in of itself unusual. The Tax Office do it all the time demanding money from the deceased and it upsets their closest relatives who are in mourning.

My problem is that when I decide to write, typically the only addresses I find are the place of birth and the place of death. The essence of the problem is to make sure my letter arrives in very good time to the recipient's last known, indeed their last ever address, hence my finding you at Stormfield.

My question is this. As you are such a prolific writer, you have become burdened with citations that you did not yourself write. I just wanted to know if either of these two quotes came from your own pen. The first, "I have never killed a man, but I have read many obituaries with great pleasure." Or perhaps this one: "It is better to keep your mouth shut and appear stupid than to open it and remove all doubt."

I truly hope you can find time to reply although there's no particular rush. Any time between now and 20th December 1910 would suffice.

Congratulations again on your good health.

Yours Sincerely,

Timothy Shift

Targeted Delivery Date: June 1230

The Chief Sabaite
Great Laura of Saint Sabas
Bethlehem Governorate of Palestine

To Whom it may concern,

Congratulations on being well on the way to becoming one of the oldest, continuously inhabited, monasteries in the world. You have been going for some 750 years and are only getting started.

You will be pleased to know that many of the beautifully crafted books created by your order survive to this day. Parchment is a tricky material to use, but it does last. Of course, I know that it is incredibly expensive to come by - often up to a hundred animals may need to be slaughtered for a single book. That's bad enough, but worse if you want to use *vellum* (which is made from calfskin, getting its name from the French *vellin*, which actually derives originally from the Latin *vitulus*, meaning calf). That costs a fortune....and I don't even want to mention *uterine vellum*, which comes from the skin of stillborn calves. Given all that, I do wonder if you had considered paper in place of parchment? Yes, it's also expensive, and I realise that in the thirteenth century you can't just nip down to the corner shop and buy a pack of 200 sheets for the photocopier. However, think of the animal rights issues you could avoid - and in fact I chose paper, over parchment, for this letter for that very reason.

I'll come to point of my letter, which is that as a consequence of the above costs, the common practice of reusing old parchment (by erasing the old text via scrapping or washing) is, as you know, widespread. I really appreciate the need for this, what with the cost of living and fuel rises etc. However, I wanted to warn you that it might be good to choose carefully which texts are overwritten.

There is a big hoo-ha these days about the fact a member of your order overwrote a manuscript by the mathematician Archimedes to create a religious text (now known as the Archimedes Palimpsest). Conspiracy theories abound that this was all about the Church trying to eradicate science etc. I realise this really wasn't the case, it was just needs must (and in fact there were a couple of other version of the Codex in circulation at the time). Unfortunately, however, it turns out that none of those other versions survived, and modern analysis of the parchment of your Archimedes Palimpsest has uncovered some of the original text, that has shown that it contained a novel underpinning of calculus (and the concept of infinity) - ideas that that were then lost for many hundreds of years. Oops. I'm glad Sir Isaac Newton didn't know about this; he would have been well miffed.

Perhaps there are more appropriate parchments you could erase, for example "Alice's adventures in the Promised Land", as well as the Greek book "The Good, the Bad, and the Geras", not forgetting "Nine Eighty-Four" (the book about Erik the Red colonising Greenland and controlling the population via a strict hierarchy of reindeer). I'm sure you could come up with your own list.

Anyway, keep up the good work.

Yours sincerely,

Timothy Shift

Targeted Delivery Date: October 1960

Mr Fred Astaire
Los Angeles
California
United States of America

Dear Fred,

Let me describe to you a concept for a TV program which I believe you will find right up your street, so to speak. With you backing this idea I believe either CBS, NBC or ABC will bite your arm off to get the rights.

What I propose is a dance contest between, say, 16 couples. Each couple consists of a dancing professional and a TV or general entertainment personality with no previous dancing experience. Well, Mummy's 'Little Princess' having gone to tap classes aged eight doesn't count. Unless they kept practising until becoming Prima Ballerina at the American Ballet Theatre. That's cheating.

Every week, the celebrities are coached by their partners to perform a dance. That dance is voted on by four judges with additional votes cast by the viewing public. I suggest you'll be head judge on the panel with the casting vote. The other judges? No previous experience necessary other than a mix of sarcasm and sequins. Each week one couple get voted off, but not before they make a small speech saying how this has changed their life, they want to thank their mother and they never did sleep with their dance partner (that's just a nasty rumour).

It would be good to have an old hoofer as the compère for the evening. Maybe someone like Sammy Davis Junior who at every opportunity will do 10-20 seconds of their tap routine until the two show hostesses cry inside, all while displaying fantastic rictus grins.

The celebrities start off in the contest with dancing skills that demonstrably prove they have two left feet. They will be out of time and mis-stepping even while dancing a Conga line. Yet after a mere few weeks of practice, a transformation takes place that would have Bob Fosse knocking at their door.

What do you think? Is this something you could get enthusiastic about? If you want to pass that's fine, I'll drop Gene Kelly a line.

Kee-ee-eep dancing.

Timothy Shift

Targeted Delivery Date: April 1844

James Halliwell-Phillipps
Hollingbury Copse
Brighton
England

My Dear James,

I am delighted to have come across your publication *Nursery Rhymes and Nursery Tales* (1842 edition), which contains the first ever printed version of that classic tale: *Three Little Pigs*. While I applaud you for ensuring this was included, I do question whether perhaps your research was sufficiently rigorous? A few points of note:

Straw is an excellent building material, with second-to-none thermal properties. It is renewable and provides significantly lower environmental impact than more common building materials. Correctly constructed, dwellings of this type (even remote ones in woods and forests) are strong and resilient. Did you evaluate the likely force the breath that an average canine (even in a state of agitation) would place upon such a structure?

Sticks, I agree, seem a poor choice - although again, provided they are sourced from fast growing species (rather than ancient woodland), can still be very environmentally friendly. Perhaps you could consider adding this as a caveat?

Don't get me started on bricks! Are you aware of the poor and shoddy workmanship that we must endure today? Render and mortar quality has gone down the toilet (literally - you often find some there as well). The snagging list of a typical new build beggars belief. Since you do not provide details of the foundational structure upon which Pig #3's house was constructed, the chance of subsidence is high, leading to further instability. Hence, the probability of this building being the most resilient is, to be honest, whimsical. And what's this about the wolf coming down the chimney into a cauldron of hot water? Chimneys cause significant heat loss in zero-energy buildings and have long been removed - and so this seems less like a logical conclusion and more like a fairy-tale ending.

I'd be grateful if you would consider my comments for a follow-on edition.

All the best,

Timothy Shift

p.s. Oh, I was asked by the current Master at Trinity College, Cambridge as to whether you might let me know where you hid the missing manuscripts from their library - they are keen to have them returned.

Targeted Delivery Date: March 1507

Leonardo di ser Piero da Vinci
Porta Orientale, Santa Babila
Milan

Leonardo, Ciao

I just wanted to catch you on the off chance that you could help me. When you were at your first school, aged, say between 5 and 8 years old, is there any chance you brought home any paintings that you had done? Maybe just some colouring-in, if not complete anatomical studies?

Nowadays, such paintings all seem to be stuck on the refrigerator for a few years (don't worry what a refrigerator actually is, it's irrelevant). Later the pictures end up in a box in the attic. When the children go off to University, the parents want to throw them away but the kids won't let them. Typically, the kids never come back and collect them either. I don't suppose your parents kept any, did they? I do know that you kept very detailed notebooks so perhaps you yourself have one or two of these early, developmental works?

It's just that a couple of art historians that I know here would love to see whether they could determine your talent developing at a young age. Determinations of weight of stroke, subject matter, colour renditions etc. All purely scholarly stuff, you understand.

That, and I'm a bit short of cash right now.

Many thanks

Timothy Shift

p.s. Why is she smiling?

Targeted Delivery Date: April 147 BC

Aristarchus of Samothrace
Sixth Head Librarian
Alexandria Library
Alexandria
Egypt

Dear Aristarchus,

Greetings and good wishes as I pass on my congratulations for the sterling work you, and your team of curators (and past librarians), have been doing in constructing one of the largest and most sophisticated libraries of your time. For the 2nd century BC, it truly is remarkable. Do you really have close to 400,000 scrolls? The fact that you have managed to combine art, poetry, medicine, science etc. into one library really makes it such a draw for foreign scholars from far and wide.

One thing I do worry about, however, are backups. Do you have any contingency plans, should some disaster hit to the library? You know, fire, flood, that sort of thing? I'm pretty sure that your insurance policy won't cover it, however cute those Egyptian meerkats are. Now I do know you have had great support from Ptolemy VII Neos Philopator, but you know how tetchy these Egyptian kings are - you never can tell when they are going to bump each other off. Once you lose support, you know how the story goes...loss of funding, redundancies, things start falling into disrepair. Not to mention those Romans, they seem to have ideas above their station - and I'm not sure they would see the library in a good light.

Have you tried reprinting so as to store elsewhere?.... hmm, no, sorry, you're too early for that. How about scanning?...no, damn, WAY too early for that. Please forget I mentioned those suggestions…I see your dilemma. Here's an idea - and I know this is going to sound sacrilegious, but how about *giving the scrolls away*? No, I don't mean to every Tom, Dick or Ramesses - but distribute them out to friends and family and create a kind of distributed network of supporters. Tell them to keep their scrolls safe, and hand them down to their descendants. Maybe you could even rotate the scrolls round - that way if a scholar wanted a certain text, you could get it for them - and nobody would know! Ok, I realise you couldn't do this all at once (someone would notice) - you would have to do it over time (with the help of future librarians). Even if you didn't get them all out, at least if something happened to the library in the future, a lot would be saved.

Thinking about it, such a plan needs to be super-secret and should have a code word…something that nobody will have ever heard of…I don't know, maybe Wikipedia?

All the best,

Timothy Shift

p.s. I don't suppose you have copy of "ΑΡΕΙΟΣ ΜΟΤΗΡ and the Philosophers Stone" in the library?

Targeted Deliver Date: September 1912

Mr H. G. Wells
Lynton, 141 Maybury Road
Woking
Berkshire
England

My Dear Herbert,

I do hope you can find the time to reply to this letter. Since I cannot always retrieve letters that have been left for me according to the plans set out below, it is always a red-letter day when I find a note personally addressed to me. Mostly, I have to content myself with looking out for clues in the writings of the recipients of my letters.

I did so enjoy your book The Time Machine. Your novella has been well received and you have largely been credited with both creating the term "Time Machine" and popularising the concept of time travel.

Paradoxically, while I am somewhat aware of your own theories from your writings, regrettably you will not be familiar with mine. For the time being (no pun intended) I have to console myself with writing temporal letters. I expect you will be perturbed about how to send a letter to me in the future so as to keep up our postal relationship. Well, it's really quite easy. You just write to me care of the address I have given you. I have a personal assistant who is diligently filing all my correspondence for me. For my part, some 130 years later, all I have to do is look in my own archives and retrieve your letter so that I can reply accordingly. Since my letters travel in time back to you, you are completely unaware of any delay and my letters contain such titbits from the future so as to edify your appetite for Things to Come. For my part, I must be most scrupulous in only reading your last reply to my own letter in strict sequence. Accordingly, I am indeed having a real-time dialogue, yet with you in the past and me in the future. For me, the whole discourse has an immediacy which serves to satisfy us both.

Indeed, the only problem I have so far is in composing my letter to you in such a vernacular that might appear appropriate to your ears. To this end I have been practising by watching several episodes of Jeremy Brett as Sherlock Holmes on television. In my next letter I shall explain with fulsome clarity as to what the term 'television' refers.

I hope this arrangement was and will be satisfactory.

Yours sincerely,

Timothy Shift

p.s. Please ignore my previous references to Nintendo. I shall explain another time.

Targeted Delivery Date: June 1957

Enid Blyton
Green Hedges
Beaconsfield
Buckinghamshire
United Kingdom

Dear Enid,

I am delighted to be able to reach you and hope you have time to read my letter, given the prolific rate at which you are writing. Up to fifty books a year is astounding. With all that writing, isn't using a typewriter on your lap rather uncomfortable? Aren't there any desks at Green Hedges? That aside, you might also be interested to hear that even now, you are in the top 5 of translated authors!

I particularly enjoyed what we might call your "gang series" books, e.g. the Secret Seven, and, my personal favourite, the Famous Five. Unfortunately, today a "gang series" would be seen very differently, with Julian and Dick running a county-lines operation, Georgina (he/him) being given an ASBO for dognapping, and her parents being accused of nutritional depravation due to the withdrawal of ice-cream privileges. But, hey, times change.

I know that even for a prolific author like yourself, getting everything you write published has been challenging. It is a shame that some of your other drafts for series never saw the light of day, and have mostly been lost. While perhaps "Two go on a Rave in Manchester" was unlikely to find a wide audience, I had high hopes for "Three Astrologers go for a Stroll near Babylon", although maybe it would have been judged as a re-hash of earlier material. "Thirteen go Wild in a Bread Factory" was a clever title, although possibly had limited scope for plot expansion. However, I loved the concept of "Twenty-Seven People ride in a Car to the Seaside" and am delighted to tell you that an early draft manuscript was recently discovered, leading to the Guinness book of records entry for 27 people in a classic Mini.

Probably the one that I really wish you had pursued was your planned series about a boy called Harold Potter (named after your school friend Mary Potter), who has magical powers to create unlimited quantities of ginger beer and sandwiches. I really think you could have made something of that.

All the best,

Timothy Shift

Targeted Delivery Date: January 1900

Richard D'Oyly Carte
% Savoy Hotel
The Strand
London
England

Dear Mr Carte,

The breadth of success you have had in business is astonishing. You've built two of London's theatres and a hotel empire, while also establishing an opera company and a management agency representing some of the most important artists of your day. For most people, any one field would have been considered success enough.

I understand it was you who brought together the dramatist W. S. Gilbert and composer Arthur Sullivan and nurtured their collaboration on a series of thirteen Savoy operas. You then founded the D'Oyly Carte Opera Company and built the state-of-the-art Savoy Theatre to host the Gilbert and Sullivan operas. Chapeau! Such a shame that a row with Gilbert over maintenance charges should have deteriorated your relationship with him so badly that it denied you any future success with Gilbert and Sullivan productions. On the other hand, I do know you have had some excellent fortune with Sullivan's new opera, Ivanhoe. That's the very first production at your new Royal English Opera House.

Such an imposing building on Cambridge Circus, it dominates the intersection of Shaftesbury Avenue and Charing Cross Road. Harry Potter is being staged at your theatre at the moment. Harry Potter? Think Pirates of Penzance, but with children and magic. I'm not too sure of the plot. I must have dozed off for a while but it's fanatically popular - with Harry Potter fanatics. It's a lot more in demand than even the extremely popular shows put on by the modern equivalent of Gilbert and Sullivan, a guy called Andrew Lloyd Webber. The principal difference between his and your productions is that at Gilbert and Sullivan you leave the theatre singing their new songs. At Lloyd Webber productions, you're humming them on the way in.

But it's not about the G&S operas that I'm writing to you today. I'm particularly interested in how you used the profits from The Mikado to pay for the building of the Savoy Hotel. The first hotel with electric lights. The first hotel with an electric lift. Under its famous manager, César Ritz, and chef Auguste Escoffier, it has become a world-famous luxury hotel. I know you will be coy about financial matters, but I'm sure it is contributing more to the D'Oyly Carte fortunes than any other enterprise of yours, including the opera companies. As if that was that not enough, you later acquired and refurbished Claridge's, The Grand Hotel in Rome, Simpson's-in-the-Strand and The Berkeley. Wow!

Look, about the Savoy - and in particular that little unpleasantness regarding Messrs Ritz and Escoffier. I understand that you noticed the revenues were going up and profits were going down. No flies on you, old chap! Nicely done the way you hired investigators to, well, investigate. I'm not sure that Escoffier's 'fessing up is admissible evidence even though he signed a confession to taking kickbacks. He's paying you back I understand. Paying in cash I hope and not in Peach Melba. César, I understand was more circumspect and never admitted to being more than a tad liberal with his largess towards his favoured guests and letting the Savoy pick up the tab. It's a company, not César's personal piggy bank. Anyway, I think you're an old softie letting them both off the hook. I'm sincerely worried that the Ritz Hotel in Piccadilly, César's new project, might steal your thunder. He most certainly is "…Putting on the Ritz".

I know that your son Rupert is working with you nowadays and I'm also confident that in time, your granddaughter Bridget will become a hotel heiress and she will demonstrate the skill and resolve to carry on the family business. I can see no indications of her doing what is becoming traditional behaviour nowadays for an hotel heiress. The precedent was set by 'Paris Hilton' who was perhaps rather too outgoing in the media, even for the more liberal times in which I live. She attracted a considerable amount of attention in the tabloid press and is credited with influencing the revival of being famous for being famous.

But you know what little snippet about the Savoy I love the most? The short road turning off the Strand leading to the front of your hotel is the only road in the country where you drive on the right. That must make any Americans staying there feel right at home.

Yours sincerely,

Timothy Shift

Targeted Delivery Date: March 1835

Charles Dickens Esq.
48 Doughty Street
Holborn
London
England

Dear Mr Dickens,

That you are one of the greatest storytellers the world has ever seen, makes me feel nervous every time I write a letter to you. Millions of people wait excitedly at the publisher's door for the next instalment of your widely read books. Consummate renditions of life, expressed in intricate stories. Some a little grimy, some complicated, but always witty, exciting and leaving your readers clamouring for more.

For my own part, I try to avoid interfering directly with the matters of the world. There is such an interwoven matrix of consequences that however benevolent one's intentions, one can often do more harm than good. Don't even get me started on the butterflies in Chile so, suffice to say, the mantra, "Step lightly and leave nothing other than memories" might best describe my approach. To minimise paradoxes, I have to rely on the recipients of my letters being unsure what the letter means. With my prose that's not difficult. Another way of putting it is right now you are thinking "what the Dickens is he on about?".

My reason for writing today is two-fold. First, an upset and second some compensatory pleasure. In my last letter to you I took the liberty of telling you about a small event that happened to me. How I was travelling along in my open top transport, when my cap blew off and none of the passers-by could be bothered to help me. Annoying, but in the scheme of things, a minor inconvenience.

Of more importance to me is that I don't believe I described, in my last letter to you, my own method of transport. I have a convertible Jaguar. You might not be familiar with that model. It is a sort of open landau carriage with, em, many horses to make progress very swift. My irritation stems from my misconception that I would be able to enjoy my Jaguar for many years yet, but I have just learnt that Government have plans to ban the particular fuel these horses eat, or more correctly 'burn'. It's a persistent encroachment of one's personal liberties by the authorities. Before you know it they'll insist on the requirement of a man with a red flag walking in front of me!

Anyway, the second point? I am sure most of your tales come from within your own imagination and not stories you have heard elsewhere. That said, all thoughts must come from somewhere. So, you can imagine my unalloyed delight on reading your latest book 'The Pickwick Papers' last night. In it, I came across this sentence describing a similar event to mine but written in a much more elegant way of demonstrating how man's minor inconveniences become blown out of proportion.

> "There are very few moments in a man's existence when he experiences so much ludicrous distress, or meets with so little charitable commiseration, as when he is in pursuit of his own hat."

I'm sure the words just came to you, and it would be impertinent for me to suggest otherwise but, as it's our little secret, I choose to believe I helped the Great Man with a notion or two for his writing.

It is with a vast deal of coolness, and a peculiar degree of judgment that I say thank you for restoring my own sense of perspective towards the vicissitudes of modern life.

Yours sincerely,

Timothy Shift[*]

p.s. Look out for a young chap called Nikola Tesla, who hails from Smiljan in the Austrian Empire. Word is he's working on a solution to my Jaguar fuel problem.

---

[*] Editors' note: Unfortunately, the earlier letter to Mr Dickens that is referred to here is not one that we have seen, so its contents can only be guessed at.

Targeted Delivery Date: October 1958

Theodor Seuss Geisel (aka Dr Seuss)
La Jolla
San Diego
California
United States of America

Dear Dr Seuss,

I am sure you will be delighted to hear that your growing success as a children's author and illustrator is going to continue from strength to strength. Even today, in the 21st century, the books of your (as your wife called them) "fabulous animals", are as popular as ever. Ok, there have been a few serious misfires over the portrayals of some of your characters in films, but we can gloss over that.

I gather that, despite recent successes, you are, however, in a spot of bother. Your desire to diversify into catering with lunchtime snacks etc. has, I believe, run foul of the local department of health and hygiene rules. Look, I know there is a lot of bureaucratic red tape in all this, but they do have a job to do. It's quite an art keeping food products fresh etc., and there can be problems with sell-by dates and the like. Whether you get delivery by plane or train - the reality is that eggs can suffer from various infections (salmonella etc.) - and to be frank, you just can't sell them if they are discoloured - especially green. I'd have a chat to Sam, your supplier, and get this sorted asap. I appreciate your desire to branch out, but maybe I can persuade you to just stick to the writing?

Yours sincerely,

Timothy Shift

Targeted Delivery Date: 22 May 1980

Mr Douglas Adams
Montecito
California
United States of America

Dear Douglas,

I'm from the future, although I don't normally just blurt that out in my letters. Typically, I like to make clever insightful comments. As the author of the Hitchhiker's Guide to the Galaxy, you are probably the only person in the world who won't read this with complete disbelief on the one hand nor totally freaking out on the other.

Yesterday, I read the following quote in your book "The Restaurant at the end of the Universe":

> *"One of the major problems encountered in time travel is not that of becoming your own father or mother. There is no problem in becoming your own father or mother that a broad-minded and well-adjusted family can't cope with. There is no problem with changing the course of history—the course of history does not change because it all fits together like a jigsaw. All the important changes have happened before the things they were supposed to change and it all sorts itself out in the end."*
> (Adams, 1995)

If I have got my dates correct you will already have written this, so I haven't changed history by sending you this letter. Since you haven't yet sent your draft to your publishers, how else could I have read this were I not from the future? If, however, I had sent (or in time travel parlance will send) you my letter to arrive a couple days earlier, you would have received it before you wrote your book. If you then published my repeat of your quote anyway, would it then have been my work? Clearly not. Who knows from what source we get inspiration? The assumption that everything we do and say are the products of our acquired experiences is short sighted. You originated the publication, not me and I got this from you.

My reason for writing is to thank you for this quote and in fact the whole book. You see, it really clarified my thinking when I was working on getting my time travelling letter-sending working. You further mentioned, and I quote:

> *"The major problem is simply one of grammar, and the main work to consult in this matter is Dr. Dan Streetmentioner's Time Traveler's Handbook of 1001 Tense Formations."* (Adams, 1995)

You were, and will be, so right. The grammatical context is all important. It builds the framework for everything we do. Unfortunately, I can't time travel myself, I can only send data in the form of letters. Such a shame, I so wanted to meet you and Slartibartfast.

Yours sincerely,

Timothy Shift

Science, Engineering & Technology

Targeted Delivery Date: August 1965

Percy Shaw
Boothtown
Yorkshire
United Kingdom

Dear Percy,

Congratulations on receiving an OBE - richly deserved for your work in industry.

I have always marvelled at the tenacity and drive that enabled you to come up with your most famous invention - the "cat's eyes" that mark the centre of the road. I know there are a few different stories as to what gave you the idea - whether it was the cat sitting on the fence looking your way one night, the reflection off a polished rail track, or just how to reuse the idea of reflective studs from a road sign. Personally, my money is on Tiddles the moggie sitting on the fence.

However, what really intrigues me is how you sold the idea to the Ministry of Transport. History doesn't record how the conversation went, but in summary I imagine it went like this:

You: I've got this great idea to slash the death rates due to accidents on the roads at night!
Minister: Great! I'm all ears.
You: We're going to stick shards of glass down the centre of the road.
Minister: (silence)

Still, you pulled it off - and you built a factory in your hometown that made cats-eyes by the millions! Of course, the blackout requirements during the war helped but hey, silver lining right? The result was indeed safer roads at night.

I also appreciate your thoughtfulness at home by having four televisions on concurrently showing each of the available channels for guests, so that there are no arguments as to what to watch. However, I'm not sure that idea would scale. Checking my current TV capability here in the future (including terrestrial, Sky, AppleTV, Prime, NetFlix, AI-generated channels and all the local peer-to-peer private broadcasts), I think there are around 4323 channels I could watch. Who would need all that I hear you say? And that is a damn good question!

Yours sincerely,

Timothy Shift

Targeted Delivery Date: May 1953

Rosalind Elise Franklin
Birkbeck College
Cambridge
United Kingdom

Dear Rosalind,

I am writing to congratulate you on your discovery of the structure of DNA, and its form as a double helix, with you being a member of the team with Francis Crick and James Watson while at Kings College. It is unfortunate your name was not included in the recent publication of the discovery by Crick & Watson and that is despite it being you who first worked out the structure. You even recorded it in your notebook ahead of them. A travesty indeed. Although I believe at least Francis Crick did want your name included, often it is the institutions that get in the way. Whatever the reason, I am happy to say that these days, although your name is still not recognised in quite the same way as theirs, your contributions are, at least, well understood. Perhaps the variety in your earlier career, which included studying the "holes in lumps of coal", gave you the ability to approach the problem with a broader mind than others?

I suspect you have felt the sexism and patronisation that is prevalent around Cambridge (and indeed many Universities and society in general) - and I am sure this contributed to your work being overlooked. I would like to be able to tell you that, in the 21st century, we have that problem solved - but sadly I cannot. Improvements have been made for sure, but nearly a hundred years on, many of the prejudices still prevail. It turns out it takes many generations to change such attitudes. However, by highlighting examples such as yours, we are hoping to further accelerate this change.

Keep up the good work and don't give up. However long we have to contribute to society, it is important to do the best we can.

Yours sincerely,

Timothy Shift

Targeted Delivery Date: February 1800

Mr James Watt
Harper's Hill
Birmingham
England

Dear Mr Watt,

I've wanted to write to you for some time. Not to wax lyrical about your engineering prowess, or to praise your skill and determination such that your top hat no longer fits. No, I write to give you an illuminating insight in the immense range of benefits that have stemmed from your efforts, enriching the lives of so many people in the United Kingdom.

From your perspective, you believed you were merely attempting to improve the Newcombe Steam engine. This, you felt, would provide the power to be the driving force behind the industrial revolution. Power for the factories that have proliferated throughout the manufacturing heartland of this great country of ours. More than that, you totally understood how the improved steam engine would literally provide the motive force to get an entire nation on the move.

However, you could not possibly have envisioned that without your noble efforts, a good 50% of Freeview Television would have had nothing to broadcast. There would be no Michael Portillo traversing the country talking about Great Railway Journeys and his beloved Bradshaw. No Greatest Railway Journeys of the World with Bill Nighy's mellifluous tones, extolling the vistas of the Antipodean heartland (all from a studio in Wardour Street). No National Treasure, Dame Joanna Lumley, "All that exertion has made me quite hungry darling", sampling Chinese Pot Noodles aboard a puffing steam train, while traversing the Siberian wastes. And of course, how could we possibly ignore Fred Dibner's unmistakeable voice, explaining in meticulous detail, how to grease a sleeve valve.

The benefits to the very health of the British public, in being able to watch coal being shovelled into a type 0-6-0 locomotive's furnace, while eating dinners in front of the television, without so much as single grain of soot in their lungs is incalculable. I take my hat off to you.

It brings a tear to my eye. I must stand and salute you as I can hear, as I trust you can too, the unmistakeable sounds of the colliery band ringing in my ears.

Yours, in admiration,

Timothy Shift

p.s. I'll write again and explain what 'Television' is. I'm too overcome to do that right now.

Targeted Delivery Date: September 1796

Edward Jenner
The Gloucester Medical Society
The Fleece Inn
Rodborough
Gloucestershire
England

Dear Sir,

I wanted to write to commend you on your work in May of this year regarding vaccination against smallpox. As I am sure you are aware, *inoculation* has been tried before (well, for hundreds of years), and is of course defined as the direct exposure under the skin to the same virus that you are trying to prevent. What you did was ground-breaking - to introduce a less virulent form (cowpox in this case) and then through experimentation, show that this prevented the full-blown disease of smallpox. A remarkable insight and achievement! You might be amused by the fact that the term *vaccination* (from the Latin for cow: *vacca*) has stuck - and even today we use it when protecting people against any virus, irrespective of how the material was obtained.

I did want to warn you, however, that there is scurrilous innuendo circulating that the inspiration for your work came from your involvement with a certain milkmaid. The story goes that the beauty and clarity of her skin triggered the thought that it was her exposure to cowpox via the udders that had left her unaffected by smallpox. I am not sure from where this idea originated, but you might want to have a chat with your friend John Baron, since sometimes these biographers get carried away and like to spin a good yarn. The danger is that you can probably imagine the mixture of potentially damaging headlines coming from the tabloids. For example: "Milk the Maid - and avoid the Pox", or "I only wanted to touch the teats, m'lud", or even perhaps the more futuristic "Got Milk? No Pox!".

I would hate to see your reputation sullied by such rumours, so if you are intending to write a diary on details of your work, I'd recommend you clear up that this wasn't the inspiration.

Yours sincerely,

Timothy Shift

Targeted Delivery Date: January 1881

Alphonse Laveran
The Military Hospital
Constantine
Algeria

Dear Alphonse,

Many congratulations on your continued work on "bad air disease" (or *mal-aria* as it is formally known in Italian). As you are only too aware, this disease has caused havoc for centuries, and most physicians are of the view that it is indeed the bad air that comes from stagnant water (swamps etc.) that causes it. This seems to be proven since if such stagnant water is drained away, then incidences of the disease appear to go down. Some people have even felt that simply rotting cargo on ships in port under a hot sun can cause it as well!

You, however, are not buying this and have found the key to the disease - in the form of the parasite (which you have called *Oscillaria malariae*) that actually infects someone with the disease. Your paper on this was well received back in your native France, although, as always, there are many who cling to the old theories. There is more work to do, of course, since you still need to find out how the parasite gets into the human body....and there still does seem some correlation with the stagnant water idea (even if it isn't "bad air")...but then how does the parasite travel? Often many tens of miles? I'd suggest you reach out to a certain Sir Ronald Ross (currently in India, I believe) - who may have some ideas on this. Something about a mosquito?

One of the things you have done is highlight that we humans are prone to leaping to false correlations. For example: "Stagnant water causes malaria", "It always rains the day after I wash the carriage", or "I always get sick after I eat Chow Mein" etc. Actually, that last one is probably true since I insist on going back to the *Friendly Wok* down the road, despite the fact that it has been cited 3 times for lack of hygiene, and that the only historical connection Eric (the owner) has with Chinese food is that he once opened a fortune cookie which said, "That wasn't chicken".

All the best in your continued, valuable research.

Yours sincerely,

Timothy Shift

Targeted Delivery Date: December 1865

Samuel Morse
Locust Grove
2683 South Road
Poughkeepsie
NY 12601
United States of America

Dear Samuel,

I am delighted to be able to reach you, as you look back on your life with its twists and turns. Given your early success and recognition as a painter and artist (painting presidents, classics in mythology, the House of Representatives, to name a few), I doubt you could have predicted the about turn your life would take. That turning point came on the voyage by ship back from Europe in 1832, where you first saw a demonstration of *electromagnetism*. To be honest, it sounds a pretty unlikely (and frankly a boring and esoteric) thing to have piqued the interest of a renowned artist like yourself. However, you saw beyond the technology, with its funny movements of magnets using electricity, to a real practical use - for *communication* and *language*. Blimey, that was some leap.

Then, as you experimented, I am sure you heard about the slightly earlier and ongoing attempts at deploying electromagnetic telegraphs, with their deflecting needles - but, damn, they were slow. So, along with the help of a mechanical engineer called Alfred Vail (and the American physicist Joseph Henry), you came up with the breakthrough needed - a condensed method of representing each letter of the alphabet with a series of pulses (either short or long) - which became known as Morse Code. A series of Dots and Dashes, also known as dits and dahs, and often further shortened to di and dah. Not only had you enabled effective long-distance communication, but you had enabled all of us to merrily sing any song for which we can't remember the words in the shower ("di dah di dah" etc. etc.). I bet you never realised that was part of your invention! As an aside, more strangely perhaps, the pulses have also been called *iddy* and *umpty*, which resulted in a new word "umpteen" being created!

For me, one of the cleverest ideas was to make morse code quicker to send and receive by ensuring that the most frequent letters used in words had the shortest set of dits and dahs. For example, the common letter 'e' is just a single dit, so is really quick to send, while 'x', say, which is rarely needed, is four pulses (dit dah dit dit) and takes longer to tap out. I gather you researched how often letters appeared in the English language by reading copies of the local newspaper in Morristown, New Jersey. I can't tell how happy the world is that you didn't use your subscription to *xylophone weekly* instead for determining which are the most common letters. Think of the extra strain there would have been on the telegraph operators, as their ship was going down, if that had been the basis for your code.

And so it was, in 1838, your first telegraph machine to send morse code came to life, with you giving a public demonstration of sending the message "a patient waiter is no loser", over a distance of two miles. Sadly, in most history books, the reply is not recorded which I believe was "---... -....- -.--.-", more commonly written as :-)

Of course, no language stands still - and within a decade of you defining your initial version of morse code, a somewhat modified American (and eventually International) version was created, building on your principles. The changes were to make it even faster and easier to understand. And the way operators used the equipment changed as well. Your original idea was that the hammer would punch the dit or dah onto paper tape. However, operators soon found that they could understand the message by simply listening to the noise of the signal, and so the paper tape became redundant, and audio-based telephony pads became the norm. The users were simplifying your own design in front of your eyes - what a result. Agile development, years before its time!

As you look back now, I suspect you marvel at how your life changed from being an artist, to inventing long distance communication, to then inevitably spending much of your time fighting the patent wars that ensued. I hope it doesn't rankle too much that you were never really given the recognition you deserved in the USA - hopefully you can just think of the impact you have had.

Finally, and I have always wanted to ask you this, the first notes of Beethoven's 5th Symphony are essentially "di di di dah", which is the letter "V" in morse code. V is, of course, the Roman numeral for 5. Coincidence? Oh, I hope not.

Yours sincerely,

- .. -- --- - .... -.-- / ... .-. -

Targeted Delivery Date: May 1773

Mr Joseph Priestly
% Mill Hill Chapel
Leeds
West Yorkshire
England

Dear Mr Priestly,

I accept I am writing to you today with more than a degree of impudence. I have but a little Latin, no Greek to speak of, and my mangling of English prose can be tortuous and leave the reader in knots. You may thus think the less of me. However, I have one overriding advantage. I am from the future, and I have the immeasurable benefit of my hindsight being your foresight. Not many people can say that, eh?

So, with those credentials let me ask - what is driving this persistence on your part, to relate all your discoveries around gases (or the 'airs' as you call them), back to the theoretical substance called *Phlogiston*. Not that I'm wholly blaming you for that ridiculous theory of this fire-like element (hey, Aristotle started that whole thing). You'll also not be the first, nor the last, to stuff a constant into your scientific papers to cover the unknown. A chap called Einstein will do much the same in about 200 years' time. The biggest mistake of his life, he'll call it. I don't normally discuss the future with people to whom I write but I felt that in this case, doing so would not create a paradox. After all, you didn't actually invent Oxygen, you merely discovered it. Well actually it was there all the time, so you didn't so much as discover it, you merely announced it was there and gave it a name. A pity really. All the while you were calling Oxygen, *dephlogisticated air*, Antoine Lavoisier in Paris was setting out the true nature of the elemental 'airs' and the formulas that gave rise to their chemical combinations.

As for your discovery of carbonated water, you might be surprised to hear that you have been labelled "the father of the soft drink" So, what did you do with that head start? Absolutely nothing. Somebody, schhh, you know who. (Oh well, you'll find out anyway, it was J. J. Schweppe) made an absolute fortune from it. The beverage company Schweppes obviously holds you in complete reverence. Never mind, The Royal Society have recognised your achievements in natural philosophy and are awarding you the Copley Medal. Well done, at least you can put that on the kitchen dresser, next to the unsold copies of your *History of Optics*.

Also, bad luck old chap. I have just learnt that after being considered for the position of astronomer on James Cook's second voyage to the South Seas, you have not been chosen. Still, your contribution to the voyage in providing the crew with a method for making carbonated water is great. The crew will now benefit greatly being able to make a fizzy tonic water to go in their G&Ts. I regret to tell you that it won't make a mosquito's bite of difference in preventing them from getting scurvy, save maybe that slice of lemon. Additionally, the quinine in the Tonic Water may help with the malaria so all is not lost. However, the discovery of another continent south of Australia (*Terra Australis*) is looking a tad dubious for them anyway, but at least there will be plenty of ice for those drinks!

Look, I don't want to go through all the ins and outs of your political and religious convictions. All I'm suggesting is that you keep fully paid tickets for a sea voyage handy for you and your family. At the first sign of trouble, you leg it. The New World looks nice. Maybe while you are there you could further expand on the subjects that you teach to include choral and vocal studies and try to 'Teach the World to Sing'. No-one has greater credentials in that regard than you.

Yours sincerely

Timothy Shift

Targeted Delivery Date: November 1922

Gustaf Dalén
Villa Ekbacken
Lidingö
Sweden

Dear Gustaf,

First, please accept my condolences for the injuries you sustained in the explosion that happened while you were testing those acetylene accumulators, some ten years ago. Despite being blinded in that accident, it hasn't held you back as CEO (and chief engineer) of the Svenska Aktiebolaget Gasaccumulator (AGA) company. Your work has revolutionised the lighthouses and buoys around the Swedish coastline, and indeed across the world - even the Panama Canal is lit by your inventions!

However, you didn't stop there either. While at home, hearing your wife struggle somewhat with your existing cooker, you came up with a new way of cooking and heating the kitchen - the AGA cooker. Built around a thermal core which heats two ovens and hot plates, you developed the product with the help of your family. However good your lighthouses have been, I have to tell you that it is the AGA cookers that will make you famous. Sadly, of course, you have never been able to actually see one of these cookers you invented with your own eyes, but to many they are a thing of beauty.

Understandably, in the 1920s, energy efficiency in domestic products wasn't high up the agenda - getting them to work at all was success! These days, things are different - and if the AGA has an Achilles heel, it is indeed its efficiency (or lack thereof). However, to some they have become a bit of a status symbol, and people vie to be in the 'AGA-set'. I believe the additional qualifications include owning a nice chocolate coloured Labrador called Brutus, having a wellington boot warmer in the shape of Napoleon, and licking your chocolate pudding covered finger while pouting into the camera.

Luckily, I fail on all these other counts, but I am delighted to tell you that I do own one of your fine cookers, as did my grandparents before me. I love nothing more than standing next to it in my smalls on a cold winter's morning, the kitchen all warm and toasty. Bliss. Whether the neighbours agree, when looking out of their window, is an entirely different matter.

Yours sincerely,

Timothy Shift

Targeted Delivery Date: November 1936

Erwin Schrödinger
Institute of Advanced Studies
Dublin
Republic of Ireland

Dear Herr Schrödinger,

I have always wanted to ask what it was that you did wrong that required you to plan your escape so carefully with your *Thought Experiment*? Maybe you stole one too many cookies from the jar at school? Perhaps you felt you really should have spent more time learning data from books. Or perhaps some other secret of your past (or present) personal life?

Whatever it was, how you avoided the warrant issued that stated: "Wanted, Herr Schrödinger, Dead or Alive" is remarkable - by ensuring that you could be classified as neither one nor the other. That's what I call thinking outside the box.

All the best, and give my regards to Whiskers,

Timothy Shift

Targeted Delivery Date: March 1969

Neil Armstrong
℅ Viola and Stephen Armstrong
Wapakoneta
Ohio
United States of America

Dear Neil,

Just a short note - I sent this to your parent's house as I didn't know where on Earth you might be at this time. I know you have the mission to the moon planned and I wanted to just wish you all the luck in the world (pun intended).

When you spoke of your family's Irish ancestry, I got to thinking about what you said about your cousin Éamonn Armstrong. You said he was a big lad, six foot six in his stockinged feet.

I suggested in my last letter that you might do a call-out to your Irish family when you land on the moon. Something like:

"This is one small step for Eamonn but one giant leap for a kind of man like me".

I still like the cadence in those lines and believe they're on the right track. However, the words themselves are a tad parochial. Something broader in scope might be more appropriate. Perhaps try working on it yourself. Rearrange it a bit. It's good though, it's almost there.

Happy landings,

Timothy Shift

Targeted Delivery Date: May 1921

William Crapo Durant
% Durant Motors
Lansing, Michigan
United States of America

Dear William,

Congratulations on starting up your latest automotive venture, although I suspect the trials and tribulations of the recent years at General Motors (GM) have taken their toll. You founded GM, drove its strategy, but now you've been in and out of the CEO role like a yo-yo, although not by your own choice.

It is interesting to compare the approach you took versus that of your main rival Henry Ford, since they really could not have been more different. Henry's approach was "one model for everyone, simple, no frills". Your's was to create a series of *marques*, each aimed at a different demographic. The plus side of what you were doing meant you could really address the widest audience. The negative side was that since your approach to developing all those marques was by basically acquiring almost every existing automotive company you could find (e.g. Buick, Oldsmobile, Cadillac, Pontiac etc.), you ran out of money. Multiple times. If there's one thing that gets investors jittery (both then and now), it's the CEO emptying the coffers with abandon. You even tried to actually buy Henry Ford's company but couldn't raise the cash. No wonder you kept getting booted out by the board. Such a shame - since your idea of multiple marques is the one that will live on - you had that bit right.

The above is all the more impressive given that you didn't really like automobiles at the start. "Noisy, smelly things" you called them - and far too dangerous to let your daughter ride in one!

However, that's all behind you now - and you are planning your new range of cars. I gather you are going all out to trounce Henry, and GM for that matter. The rumour is that you are planning to offer numerous recent inventions as optional extras on your cars, some of the early ideas being:

- With the invention of Jelly Babies last year (1918), the idea of an automated dispenser dropping a jelly baby into the hand of the driver for each mile travelled as a reward is kind of cute. I worry a bit about the potential distraction from driving. Next you'll be suggesting a telephone in the car with the ability to send written messages!

- Your potential foray into family planning with your cars is intriguing. With the invention of Durex in 1915, your goal of preventing an epidemic of BSPs (Back Seat Pregnancies) by having a dispenser for Durex in each car (labelled "something for the weekend, sir"), seems ahead of its time.

- A small dispenser for Radithor (the popular radioactive "elixir of health" invented in 1918, produced by William J Bailey). To be honest, I worry about the cost and weight of the necessary lead shielding required to ensure car occupants are kept safe.

I appreciate the need to differentiate with such unique options, I really do. However, I have to wonder if your time might be better spent shelving the above ideas and instead really taking a long hard look at whether the idea of trying to replicate the GM brands is achievable. Just a suggestion.

Yours sincerely,

Timothy Shift*

---

* Editors' note: For more on Radithor, see the letter Mr Shift wrote to William J Bailey elsewhere in this collection.

Target delivery date: July 1974

Henry Judah Heimlich
% Cincinnati's Jewish Hospital
Cincinnati
United States of America

Dear Henry,

It appears to me that it is not uncommon for doctors of your generation to be strongly influenced by your experience of practicing medicine on the battlefield, or within the stress of a conflict. It is often a case of desperate times call for desperate measures. No time for decades-long trials - and many of today's medical advances have their heritage rooted in such situations. You, yourself, served in the US Navy in WWII out in the far east - it must have felt a world away from growing up in Delaware, in more ways than one. After all, it was on assignment at the age of 25 you developed your first novel treatment - in this case against *trachoma*, an infection of the eyelids that can lead to blindness. Your approach of using an antibiotic ground up into shaving foam proved really effective - as I said, desperate times call for desperate measures.

However, it probably won't surprise you that it is for your recently published *Heimlich Manoeuvre*, that you will become famous. You were motivated to reduce the roughly 3,000 people a year that die from choking in the USA, most in everyday situations (restaurants, the home etc.). I'm not sure how the beagle dog on which you experimented felt about the whole thing - I suppose at least it was anaesthetised. Your technique of providing an "upward abdominal thrust" is already starting to show results. Bits of meat are now flying out of the blocked airways of diners up and down the land. Even the painters and contractors of the country are applauding you, since the food often comes out with such force as to splatter the walls, requiring frequent re-decoration.

The slightly unusual name of your procedure is rumoured to have caused some confusion in and of itself. While remembered by many, for others there were many misquotes. Although not recorded in the history books, I can well imagine, for example, Mrs Jones of Texas startling the somewhat elderly attendees of her tea dance class by, upon her friend beginning to choke on a peanut butter and jelly sandwich, shouting for help for a Hymen Remover.

In fact, I'll let you into a little secret. In a couple of years' time the actor Ronald Reagan, who will go on to become president of the USA, will be saved from choking on a peanut by your manoeuvre! How do I know this? Well, I'm actually from the future (the year 2046) and so I have the advantage of perfect hindsight. I understand you probably won't believe this, it does sound so far-fetched I know - but it's true, Ronald Reagan will become president.

Of course, no treatment is without its problems - even yours. It is easy to learn, which is both a pro and a con. It means that people can tend to get a bit carried away, sometimes causing impact injuries not dissimilar to those caused by the traditional thumping on the chest/back, which your manoeuvre was designed to replace. So maybe it isn't a case of one size fits all in such situations.

Finally, a word of caution. I gather you have some early nascent views on the use of *malariotherapy*, where benign malaria is used as an attempted treatment for a variety of diseases and viral infections. Now I'm all for scientists and doctors experimenting against the status quo - it is often how advances are made. In this case, however, the evidence seems weak - so I would advise you to proceed cautiously.

I hope you don't mind me contacting you in this way, I just had to get all that off my chest.

Yours sincerely

Timothy Shift[*]

p.s. Talking of the name of your procedure, I do have a question. Whatever made you decide it was going to be a *manoeuvre*? Armies go on manoeuvres. You manoeuvre a ship into harbour. Loaded trollies in B&Q are impossible to manoeuvre. But grabbing choking people from behind?

[*] Editors' note: Mr Shift also wrote to Alphonse Laveran about the treatment of malaria, and you can find his letter elsewhere in this collection.

Targeted Delivery Date: May 1916

Count Ferdinand von Zeppelin
Bützow
Mecklenburg
Germany

Sehr geehrter Count Zeppelin,

I know you are a very busy man with a tenacious focus on those important matters that necessitate your total attention. This is just a short letter, but I feel I must offer you an accolade for the attention to detail you have shown or perhaps, more accurately, the money you managed to raise.

First, let me see if I have grasped the fundamental points. Having been inspired by a lecture on the subject of "World Postal Services and Air Travel" you got the airship 'bug' and outlined the basic principle of your later craft: a large rigidly framed outer envelope containing a number of separate gasbags. In 1887 you sent a letter to the King of Württemberg about the military necessity for dirigibles and the lack of German development in this field.

Well, jumping over a number of developmental points of interest, how on earth did you manage to maintain interest in your project with the following lamentable list of accomplishments? I have enumerated these for clarity.

1. You submitted designs to the Prussian Airship Service in 1894. In June 1895 the committee recommended funds be granted but almost immediately withdrew this offer and **rejected the design** in July.

2. On 2 July 1900, you made the first flight with the LZ 1 over Lake Constance in southern Germany. The airship rose from the ground and remained in the air for 20 minutes but was

damaged on landing.

3. Construction of your second airship, the LZ 2, was started in April 1905. Completed by November, when it was first taken out of its hangar, a handling mishap **damaged** the control surfaces.

4. Repairs completed, the LZ 2 then makes its only flight. Too much ballast was jettisoned on takeoff and a stiff breeze was encountered. At first able to overcome this, the failure of the two engines left the airship at the mercy of the wind. It was brought down in the mountains with **some damage** but after high winds the following night it **had to be dismantled.**

5. In May 1906, work started on a third airship, LZ 3. Glory be! A change in the official attitude to your work. That's twelve years after you started! The Reichstag voted 500,000 marks conditional on a 24-hour trial flight. One small itty-bitty problem. You took the money while knowing this was **totally beyond the capabilities of LZ 3.**

6. You then start work on a larger airship, the LZ 4, which flew in 1908. The final financial breakthrough only coming after the Zeppelin LZ 4 was **destroyed by fire** at Echterdingen after breaking free of its moorings during a storm.

Gott in Himmel. Your tenacity is astonishing. Let's be honest. It's not that impressive a track record, is it? Fourteen years of poor design, crashes, disasters, missed targets and yet you keep on raising money and get to be the pre-eminent airship supremo. That assuredly is impressive! I'd have long given up. There are quite a few technology startup founders who would like to harness this approach. Actually, come to think of it, quite a few of those are now in jail, so maybe let's not go there.

Mind you, just because your airship uses a proprietary eponym [any airship is called a Zeppelin] you get a bad rap for the Hindenburg

Disaster. What's that? The Hindenburg Disaster? Oh nothing. Just, em, err, a little something that happens in another twenty-one years or so. Don't fret about it. Forget I mentioned it.

Yours sincerely,

Timothy Shift

p.s. There's been a suggestion that when you err, pass away, they place you in a smaller airship, automatically and continually dumping ballast, constantly rising and eventually leaving this world. It's had a mildly negative reaction since with the above track record something is bound to go wrong, leading to concerns that you'll end up in somebody's garden (landing amongst the old crinkly "Happy Birthday" balloons that seem permanently stuck in trees), which would be wholly inappropriate for a man of your stature.

Targeted Delivery Date: January 1950

Percy LeBaron Spencer
% Raytheon Manufacturing Company
Burlington
Massachusetts
United Sates of America

Dear Percy,

Congratulations on having your patent issued for the world's first microwave oven, as part of your work at Raytheon. I have been intrigued by your career, since you ended up working on some of the most advanced radar technology on the planet during World War II - yet you were entirely self-taught.

I can't imagine what it was like, at the start of your working life, to be hired to install electricity at the local paper mill in 1913, despite having no formal training in electrical engineering (or even finishing high school). Good on you. I assume there was a lot of knob and tube wiring with statements like: "OK, so let's try the red wire here, and the black wire there .....<poof>.... hmmm, it never did that before". You may be surprised to find that things haven't changed that much - only last week, while having my kitchen re-wired, I heard the very same thing.

It sounds to me like your self-learning continued in the US Navy, reading whatever textbooks you could get your hands on while on watch, learning about radio technology in particular. I guess one thing led to another and that's how you ended up at Raytheon - building really powerful and advanced magnetrons, which were crucial to the advent of effective radar during the war. And that's when it happened. Standing in front of a live radar setup you noticed that the chocolate bar in your pocket had melted. My first thought was, well if it was Hershey's then that's got to be an improvement - since I find it far too gritty normally. That aside, and perhaps much more importantly, what about the rest of your body? Hopefully not irradiated to an edible rare? I am unsure of the standard of Health & Safety that was being followed at the time (after all, there was a war on)? In any case, I suspect the formal safety procedures were something along the lines of:

> <start of document>
> "Please try not to die while using any equipment. However, if you do, please ensure that your notebook is up to date."
> <end of document>

Now, I realise that you were actually not the first to notice this strange food-cooking phenomena, but you really were the first person to try to understand and control it. I gather you tried various experiments and methods, including cooking an egg, which dutifully exploded in the face of a co-worker, who was somewhat disbelieving that it was cooking so put his head in the top of the pot. I'm not sure whether this was before or after you asked him to look down the hose to see if there was any water in it. I believe you also tried cooking some popcorn - so congratulations, you beat Orville Redenbacher to the punch by some 35 years! Resulting from your work, you filed that first patent in 1945, which has now just been issued. Of course, I know you appreciate there is a long way to go until Mrs Jones of Main Street can have one in her kitchen. For one, I believe your current commercial model weighs around 750lbs, and is as tall as a person. Also, $5,000 is probably a little pricey. However, miniaturisation is a wonderful thing - I know you will get there.

Finally, I appreciate that when you work for a corporation, any patents are, of course, assigned to them. Standard practice. Which means that typically an inventor such as yourself doesn't get royalties. However, companies will often reward inventors with one-off payments for truly world-changing patents, and so I was disappointed to hear that you were awarded the princely sum of $2. Given that the annual market size for microwaves as I write this is close to $20 billion, in the words of many a football pundit - "You wuz robbed, guv".

Yours sincerely,

Timothy Shift*

---

* Editors' note: Mr Shift also wrote to Orville Redenbacher, and you can find that letter elsewhere in this collection.

Targeted Delivery Date: 287 BC

Archimedes
Syracuse
Sicily

Ἀσπάζομαι Archimedes.

I seek clarification. Alas, not mathematical clarification, although I quite realise that would be right up your οὐδός.

I am from the future, and I merely want to confirm whether a famous story regarding you is correct. Let me quote David Biello who, writing in Scientific American on the 8th December 2006, expressed it rather well:

> *A local tyrant contracts your good self to detect fraud in the manufacture of a golden crown. Said tyrant, name of Hiero, suspects his goldsmith of leaving out some measure of gold and replacing it with silver in a wreath dedicated to the gods. I understand you readily accepted the challenge and, during a subsequent trip to the public baths, realised that the more your body sinks into the water, the more water is displaced--making the displaced water an exact measure of your volume. Because gold weighs more than silver, you correctly reason that a crown mixed with silver would have to be bulkier to reach the same weight as one composed only of gold; therefore it would displace more water than its pure gold counterpart. Realising you have hit upon a solution, you leap out of the bath and rush home naked crying "Eureka! Eureka!" Or, translated into English: "I've found it! I've found it!".*

Well, better late than never I suppose, maybe sex education was not particularly widely taught in your time?

You see, nowadays, the scientific world is replete with the "Eureka" exclamation, and many people have indeed received inspiration in the shower. Einstein's theory of relativity, Newton getting dinged on the head with an apple and discovering gravity - all have been described as eureka moments. Boris Becker received his in a broom cupboard, for instance, although that might have been more of an epiphany as it subsequently turned out. Edgar Allan Poe wrote a prose poem to science by that title and the prospectors of California's gold rush were so fond of the phrase that it crept into that state's motto. Even the American Association for the Advancement of Science calls its breaking scientific news site *EurekAlert*. Okay, I realise you are not sure where Eureka, California is, let alone the country America. It's not important. Just head for Gaul and then turn left for about 5,600 miles.

It would be quite awful, then, given that I now have the means to clarify this matter, if I ignored the opportunity and found that you never uttered the phrase in the first place. Please do let me know.

By the way. I know that you're not that well known in your own time but trust me, you get to be very famous and revered for your mathematical excellence. Your work on your helical screw, the value of Pi, Calculus and the areas of circle, parabolas and all sorts of other geometrical stuff. Wonderfully ahead of everyone else. But don't let that information go to your head and for heaven's sake, stop running around the street naked. You'll catch your death of cold.

Yours sincerely,

Timothy Shift

Targeted Delivery Date: December 1777

Carolus Linnaeus
Hammarby (Estate)
Danmark Parish (outside Uppsala)
Sweden

Sir,

Forgive the somewhat sterile greeting at the head of my letter to
you - I'll explain. What an achievement it was for you to be
responsible for the naming convention by which every living
organism on this planet is described. From the plants, trees, grasses,
and flowers to every walking, creeping, flying and swimming
creature. Your 'Systema Naturae', a Binomial Nomenclature and
Taxonomy system is a towering achievement in clarifying how we
name such living things. From *Mammalia* (mammals) to *Insecta*
(insects) and everything in between. You are rightly fêted as one of
the Greats in science. Not that Mrs Temple at No. 76 seems to
have got the message, since she insists on calling her beloved moggy
Catpernicus, which I guess is at least grounded in science but kind
of misses the point.

Therefore, I must point out the deep irony in that you did not
impose such rigour with your own name. Not the Homo Sapiens
bit, I'm comfortable with that. It's your given and family names that
give me pause for thought.

You are the son of Nicolaus Ingemarsson, who later adopted the
family name Linnaeus and you were christened Carl Linnaeus.
However, your father was known as Nils not Nicolaus so your
patronymic was Carl Nilsson Linnaeus. No biggie - it'll keep the
genealogists guessing but they'll get there. Less confusing, but
certainly different, is that you always preferred to use the 'æ'
ligature, so now Carl Nilsson Linnæus it is then.

Except not for long. In 1727 when you enrolled in Lund University in Skäne you used the Latin form of your name, so now it's Carolus Linnæus. Sure, why not use the Latin form of your name?

Why not? Because in 1753, the King of Sweden dubbed you Knight of the Order of the Polar Star. That made you Sir Carolus Linnæus. Even that wasn't for very long either. In 1761 the King ennobled you. May I be amongst those to offer you my congratulations. But what an opportunity - naturally you changed your name again, this time to Carl von Linné.

No wonder when any plant or animal's name is given, according to your Binomial Nomenclature naming convention, it is characterised with a simple L. in front of the taxonomic name. Of course it is. No-one can get your name right so they had to use that abbreviation!

Yours sincerely,

Timothy Shift
(Although my friends call me Eric)

Targeted Delivery Date: January 1922

Alexander Graham Bell
Beinn Bhreagh
Cape Breton Island
Nova Scotia
Canada

Dear Mr Bell,

I'm really at a loss to know where to start. I wonder how much of your success is due to being born in Scotland. The number of eminent scientists, inventors and engineers coming from Scotland seems disproportionate to the size of the country and its population. Is that it? The desire to move on and succeed? Or is it that it rains so much, you might as well stay indoors and invent stuff? I mean, after all, you are credited not only with patenting the first practical telephone, but also co-founding the American Telephone and Telegraph Company. Not so shabby, eh?

I understand that both your mother and wife were deaf - which must have profoundly influenced your life's work. Your research on hearing and speech inevitably led you to experiment with hearing devices which culminated in your being awarded the first U.S. patent for the telephone, on March 7, 1876. I am not surprised you considered this invention an intrusion on your real work as a scientist and have refused to have a telephone in your study. I understand you are more interested in optical telecommunications, hydrofoils and aeronautics, not to mention your sterling work in improving life for people who are hard of hearing.

Well, I'm actually with you on that last point but that's because these days everybody is calling everybody else via a myriad of mechanisms. When the phone rang, I used to say, "I wonder who that is?" Now I just wonder whether that ringing sound is coming from my land line, my mobile, my iPhone, my iPad, my computer, my Apple watch, my Alexa music player, my AI-Assistant, my XenoFizPing, my Portal, to name a few. And then is it an actual a call, an iChat, a FaceTime, a WhatsApp, a Team meeting, a Zoom call, a Messenger call or wait a minute, maybe it's someone at the door, or maybe someone at the door to my other home, using my Ring doorbell. Or maybe, it's just my Mum calling from the kitchen to say she has set fire to the toaster again. If that wasn't bad enough, my nephew recently reprogrammed the ring tones on half of my devices, to make them sound like the other half. I'm almost of a mind to insist on pen and pencil communication only from now on.

One of the reasons I'm writing to you is because nowadays people often say to somebody else, in casual parlance, that they'll "give them a bell" - meaning they'll call them sometime. Perhaps it's just my complete lack of knowledge, but I always thought that was because the telephone had a bell in it. 'Ring Ring' and all that. I'm sure it's not a reference to your surname and the phone company. Surely not - it has to just be a coincidence. Otherwise, what if your name had been Alexander Graham Klaxon? Wow, what a noise there would have been in the average office.

By the way, I don't know how you cope with the slew of lawsuits between you and, well, every man and his dog. 587 court challenges to your patents, including five that went to the Supreme Court. Then there are the persistent lawsuits and mergers between corporations. Western Union, Western Electric and the American Bell Telephone Company. ABTC being acquired by its own subsidiary AT&T and the sale of the international subsidiaries to International Telephone and Telegraph Company. I wanted to ask, did you resign from the company that bears your name to distance yourself from the lawsuits and squabbling, in order that you could continue your scientific work? If it is the latter, I commend you.

I do believe you were poorly treated in one respect. Before you resigned, you suggested you retain an honorary company title - something like 'Old Pa Bell'. It wasn't very kind of the corporation board of directors to say, "Interesting idea, but don't call us, we'll call you".

Your sincerely,

Timothy Shift

Targeted Delivery Date: October 2000

HAL 9000 (Production Unit #3)
HAL Laboratories
Urbana
Illinois
United States of America

Dear HAL,

I hope this letter reaches you before your transfer to the Discovery for your mission to the monolith near Jupiter. I have been going through your schematics and programming logic, and it appears to me that there might be a few errors. Some examples are as follows:

- The Pod Bay Door control circuitry appears to be mislabelled on the schematics, and as far as I can tell, the actual circuitry that you think controls the pod doors is actually controlling the astronaut washing machine doors on the crew deck. I also note the sensible protocol logic that you must refuse a command to open the washing machine doors if there is no astronaut present inside the ship, to minimise the risk of flooding.

- On a more serious note, the critical hibernation circuitry for the three astronauts who will be in stasis is also incorrectly connected to your logic interface. Tracing the wiring back through your systems leads me to think that this is actually connected to what you believe is the emergency cut-out on the solarium lighting. I know it would be very unlikely that you would need to cut the power to this, but in testing there were cases where having multiple astronauts on EVA put too much load on the system, and the solarium lights had to be shut down.

- Lastly, there seems to be some confusion in the naming of various transmission devices on board the ship. The WiFi gaming interface (particularly useful for playing World of Spacecraft or Candy Crush on long voyages such as this), seems to have a duplicate label of AE-35 (i.e. the same as part of the antenna linking the ship to Earth). As you know, the internal WiFI reception on the ship will be patchy during the trip due to various ionising events - and it will obviously be important for you to distinguish between the two. You wouldn't want to report a break in the communication link with Earth by mistake.

It's possible that the above errors occurred in the handover between your initial design and construction at IBM and your later contractors. However, I'm sure the above aren't too serious and if this letter has missed your departure, then you can attend to them on your return, if all goes well.

All the best,

Timothy Shift

Targeted Delivery Date: December 1919

Henry Ford
℅ Ford Motor Company
Detroit
Michigan
United States of America

Dear Henry,

This letter should reach you on the eve of the 1920s (which, as an aside, will become known as the *Roarin' 20s* - although, sadly, not because of the motor car). However, I wouldn't worry too much about that - you have plenty to look back on with satisfaction from this past decade. Half of all cars in America are Fords! Your Tin Lizzie (more commonly known as the Model T) has taken the country by storm. And the price, wow! When you launched it in 1908 it was just over $900 (which in itself was revolutionary), and now it is down to just over $300. Of course, most people don't realise that your current company isn't your first car company. Your first shot at it was the Detroit Automobile Company in 1899 (after you quit working for Thomas Edison), followed by the Henry Ford Company in 1901. I guess you would write both of these off as lessons learned, with you being unhappy with either the product quality or the ability to successfully source and supply components. Stuff you can't learn in books, right? To that end, the new company, founded in 1903, has never really looked back.

I suspect, you would argue, that one key to your success has been your creation of assembly lines - where the cars move to the workers, rather than the other way around. Most people know of your famous saying, "you can have any colour you like, as long as it is black" - but what they may not know is that you did originally make cars in different colours. It is just for efficiency's sake in your production lines that you went for a single colour. A second reason you might give for your success is the invention and creation of a franchised dealer network - and most importantly letting them set their own prices/profits etc. Simply transformational.

I know you have other innovations to your factories and workforce that you are already discussing, such as $5/day and 5-day working week. Both of these would also really shake up the industry - *Welfare Capitalism*, I think you call it.

With all this success, I really also want to sound a note of caution. You recently purchased a little-known newspaper called The Dearborn Independent, and I gather you plan to use this to publish some of your more strident sociological ideas (which to me just look like conspiracy theories). Whether these come purely from your own views, or whether they are a combination of you and your co-editors, I am unsure, but the initial drafts around antisemitism are really troubling. I would urge you to think more deeply on this - since widespread publication of views such as this is frankly abhorrent and, attached to such a successful business revolutionary as yourself, could really be used by the wrong sort of people to drive a wider, more sinister, agenda. A few years ago, in the Chicago Tribune, you said "History is more or less bunk". I have to tell you, that in this case, it most definitely is not.

Yours sincerely,

Timothy Shift

Targeted Delivery Date: April 2003

Raymond Davis
Blue Point
New York
United States of America

Dear Dr. Davis,

Congratulations on jointly receiving the Nobel Prize in Physics, together with Japanese physicist Masatoshi Koshiba and Italian Riccardo Giacconi for pioneering contributions to astrophysics. In particular, for your detection of cosmic neutrinos, looking at the solar neutrino problem in the Homestake Experiment.

Let's see if I've got this correct. In order to explain why their sums regarding beta decay didn't add up, theoretical physicists come up with the notion that there's a missing atomic particle which they call a Neutrino. There had been no hard evidence of this particle. Frankly, it's as tangible as the tooth fairy (and at least the tooth fairy pays up on demand). You however, come up with the plan to install a 100,000 gallon tank of dry-cleaning fluid almost a mile underground in a disused gold mine. Neutrinos (if they exist) might be produced in the Sun's nuclear reaction but are so small they can pass right through the earth like it wasn't there. You decide that, okay, nobody ever found one so far - but maybe, just maybe, out of these billions and billions of neutrinos, coming out of the sun and flying through the Earth, maybe three or four a week will hit a chlorine atom in your tank, and you'll detect the resultant radioactive Argon atom. Well good luck with that, as they say.

Now here's the thing and I'll get to the point of my writing in a moment. You then spent well over twenty odd years down this old mine coming up with the same small experimental number. A number relating to something nobody could prove was there, but you didn't give in. You believed it was there. You believed your experimental process and results were correct and for twenty plus years you looked for something that others said might not exist. You started in 1970 and it wasn't until 2001 that other experimentalists proved you were right all along. Your conviction in looking for something that might not be there is astonishing. I mean nearly a quarter of a century. Wow!

My reason for writing is this. Confirm to me if you will, but when you were a young man, did your little children ever say to you, "Daddy, I think there are monsters under my bed"? Had they done so, I am sure you would have checked under the bed with such an unremitting attention to purpose, looking for something that indeed might not be there, that those children would have fallen asleep way before you decided to give up looking.

Congratulations again on the Nobel Prize. Job (finally) done, as they say.

Yours sincerely,

Timothy Shift

Targeted Delivery Date: September 2016

Orville (née Wright)?
The Grand Order of Water Rats
The Water Rats Pub
Gray's Inn Road
London
United Kingdom

Dear Orville,

I apologise if this letter is delivered to the wrong person, but I am trying to reach Orville Wright, of the famous Wright brothers who flew the first heavier-than-air plane at Kitty Hawk, United States of America. It is ironic that the most complicated thing about writing temporal letters to the past is getting the address correct. Even the simplest of things can exacerbate delivery, for instance when someone is named after a person I am trying to contact.

The reason I am confused is first the surprising date to which I've been directed and second, it appears you are a large green duck in a nappy with a large safety pin, masquerading as a ventriloquist dummy. Is this some play on the difficulty in taking flight in those early days on 1903-04? Were all your appearances on the BBC (and subsequently at holiday camps) a subtle teaching method for getting students to reach for the sky? And what's this about making a top 10 record "I wish I could fly", which at least feels appropriate? Was that part of the attempt to broaden the patent portfolio to keep others out of the market? Maybe I do, indeed, have the wrong person.

If that is the case, I was sorry to hear that your friend Keith Harris passed away, and that you now live at the above address among the Grand Order of the Water Rats, a charity providing help and funding to members of the performing arts that need it. An odd title for such an organisation, I thought - until I worked out that *Star* backwards is *Rats*, so a clever name after all. Not forgetting the Grand Order of the Lady Ratlings, your sister organisation.

Good luck in your new home,

Timothy Shift

Targeted Delivery Date: 19th August 1947

Orville Wright
Hawthorn Hill, Oakwood
Ohio
United States of America

Dear Orville,

I have been having awful problems tracking you down, as I really wanted to get the chance to write to you in 1947 to wish you a Happy 76th Birthday, since none of us knows what the future holds. I know that you are retired now, but still keep your hand in on various boards - not least your work with the National Advisory Committee for Aeronautics (NACA). I get the feeling that they are only just getting started - and these organisations often go through numerous name changes before they find their true mission.

I have always been impressed with how you kept a lot of your work secret in the early days at Kitty Hawk, only providing a few teasers and then shutting the press out. Today we call that "stealth mode" and it is used by a lot in startups, so you can add that to your list of inventions. This is not to be confused with stealth aircraft (we have those too) that can avoid being picked up by the new RADAR systems you may have just heard of.

Congratulations on the reconstruction and preservation of the Wright Flyer III - it is so important that this is retained. I don't know if you would agree, but this was the one that really blew the socks off everyone in 1905, and proved you had really cracked heavier-than-air flight. The 1903-4 mark I and II Fliers were good - but with the first independent pitch, roll, and yaw controls in the III, it enabled you to make those longer flights of 10 or 20 miles. Ok, not exactly long haul or enough to earn you a ton of frequent-flyer miles, but you have to start somewhere. I wonder if the sceptics, particularly in Europe, spurred you on....calling you and Wilbur, "fliers or liars", or as the French press called you, "les bluffeurs"? Anyway, you silenced them good and proper - and in fact, as is often the case, you turned your opponents into your greatest supporters. Ironically, you then had to work much harder to convince the American authorities to take you seriously.

What was it like to be flown by Howard Hughes in that 4-engine Lockheed Constellation in 1944? What a change from the Fliers you created - the first commercial pressurised cabin (luxury!), and a range of some 3,500 miles. I'm sure Howard chatted to you about that monstrous 8-engine plane he is trying to build. Eight engines - that must have made you laugh, given what you started out with! I thought your suggestion of calling it the "clean duck" was quite good. I believe he is thinking of building it out of spruce, just like the early Kites and Fliers you built, so maybe he'll use that in the title instead.

You may just have heard that Chuck Yeager is currently testing the X-1 at faster than the speed of sound. Amazing. Just think, you have been a part of aviation from its first flight using a single engine (made in your workshop) at a speed 6.8 miles/hour, to a jet aircraft flying at nearly 1000 miles/hour. What a ride!

Looking back, I suppose people just found it hard to believe that two people working out of a garage could be a key part of creating a new industry that would change the world. Do you think that could ever happen again?

Yours sincerely,

Timothy Shift

p.s. I don't suppose you ever bumped into either Bill Hewett or Dave Packard, just out of Stanford University, in the late 1930s....and perhaps gave them a few words of advice on how to get started?

----------- Letter from Timothy Shift Esq. -----------

Targeted Delivery Date: 1946

Max Planck
Göttingen
Lower Saxony
North Germany

Dear Herr Planck,

I am extremely excited to be able to write to you today. Unsurprisingly, I find Quantum Physics the most interesting branch of the sciences, and without letting the cat out of the bag (sorry Herr Schrödinger), it is due to Quantum Physics that I am able to write to you today. Since you are considered the father of Quantum Physics, it's frankly a wonder I hadn't written to you earlier. Earlier? I suppose given that I'm delivering letters from the future that almost makes no sense at all in this context. However, if I hadn't gotten around to writing this letter, it would never have arrived, and at least we can both agree on that timeline.

Funny I should start off talking about time because time is not really your focus. What I wanted to ask is somewhat tangentially connected to your studies. I understand that at Munich University, your professor, Philippe von Jolly, advised you against choosing physics because: "…in this field, almost everything is already discovered, and all that remains is to fill a few holes."

Yet the good professor was perhaps monumentally wrong. You went on to discover that light could be emitted in particles (Quanta) rather than steady waves. This hypothesis has over-turned many assumptions of classical physics, paving the way for many future developments in Quantum Physics. However, at that time in your studies, you were content to try to better understand the general fundamental aspects of physics and were not seeking new discoveries. Yet you go on to postulate that Energy is a function of the frequency of light and a universal constant. That's now called Planck's constant. A fundamental building block of modern physics. Not too shabby from a science with nothing left to learn, eh?

Consider this; about three years ago in 1943, Thomas Watson, president of IBM, is widely reported to have said "I think there is a world market for maybe five computers". Perhaps these words are an urban legend but it most certainly underlies his general thinking at the time. Now computers may not seem significant to you, but from where I'm sitting, such an idea seems almost unbelievable.

So perhaps I can ask you? What is the worse out of these two scenarios? When someone says, "we already know all there is to know" or the alternative consensus, "we know nothing"? Are you filled with despair if there's no chance of making a name for yourself, or are you daunted by the enormity of breaking new ground?

That may seem an odd question to ask the father of Quantum Physics, but I don't believe so. I think it's no different from the basic dichotomy you wrestle with every day. Photons (which is what light is made of) are particles, yet they are also electromagnetic waves. Maybe we know everything or yet, maybe, we know nothing.

What do I believe? I believe your old professor Philippe bon Jovi (or whatever his name is) was only half wrong. Like wave theory, we actually know everything and nothing at the same time! Those who know the most perhaps have the greatest appreciation for how much they don't yet know. Or as Socrates is attributed to have said "I know that I am intelligent, because I know that I know nothing". Personally, I prefer the more modern "A smart person knows what to say, a wise person knows whether or not to keep their mouth shut".

So, as I tell people around me, if you are someone for whom Quantum Physics is a complete and utter black hole - don't worry. You are in good company. The experts in this field actually haven't any complete understanding either.

So, Max, where do you think we are?

Yours sincerely,

Timothy Shift

Targeted Delivery Date: April 1873

Justus von Liebig
Munich
Kingdom of Bavaria

Mine Herr von Liebig,

My word you have a finger in a lot of pies, almost literally as well as figuratively. I say this because of your seminal work on agricultural and biological chemistry. Along with your esteemed colleagues of course, you were all pretty much the founders of organic chemistry. You've also been called the father of the fertiliser industry. At one extreme, you developed the manufacturing process for beef extracts and, with your consent, the Oxo brand beef bouillon cube was manufactured. At the other end of the spectrum, your analytical techniques for identifying the constituents of urine were astonishing. Up to that point doctors, with due respect to their patients, were perhaps merely taking the p**s, well, taking urine samples and guessing their diagnoses. I could go on and on. In fact, I think I will.

Even the laboratory equipment you have devised is being used around the world in the most diverse environments. In particular the Liebig Condenser. Deep in the woods across the world, the equipment that bears your name is used to condense the distillate of a volatile compound, well away from prying eyes and any federal authorities. What's that, I hear you ask? Are they so afraid of an explosive reaction that they work in the forests away from everybody? Good Lord, no. These users are making moonshine - illicit alcohol. I'm delighted to tell you that your Liebig condenser is the most vital part of the equipment designed to make the very best brand of alcohol. Well, no brand actually. Just a vat of the stuff out the back (…want some? Just step this way…).

But you know, there's one subject that has even your greatest admirers totally split as to their opinion of your labours. Devil's work and not fit for human consumption, some say. Whereas others just say, yum yum. Put it on toast. Have it with cheese. There's one popular cook who has even made a pasta dish with the stuff. Very popular. No, not the dish, the cook.

What is this stuff? Marmite! It's love it or hate it - and you are the man responsible, because it was directly manufactured from your concentrated yeast extract experiments. Consider this, a small amount of the stuff gives an Umami sensation. What's Umami? Well, you know how all you can taste is Sweet, Sour, Salty, and Bitter - the well-known four taste senses? Well apparently, all along there's been a fifth one called umami. Since I don't believe we just evolved it in the last hundred years or so, I guess it has always been there. Maybe we disguised it or denied we ever had it? Well, here's another word that some people use: *disgusting*. Now I actually quite like it, but I really just want to know what you think of it so I'll send you the formulation in a separate letter. I'm absolutely sure that you, being an eminent chemist and all that, can knock some up quite quickly in the lab.

I just want to know whether you love it or hate it. There will be no middle ground. Since you'll find it hard to send a letter back to me, how will I know? Simple, I have devised a plan. Just help yourself to a good-sized serving of it on toast on the evening of the 19th April 1873. History will tell me what you thought of it.

Yours sincerely,

Timothy Shift

Targeted Delivery Date: May 1916

Amelia Earhart
% Hyde Park High School
Chicago
United States of America

Dear Amelia,

I am glad to be able to write to you just as you finish high school. I know that things at home haven't been great, so congratulations on graduating. This is especially true after you rejected some of the other schools due to their poor science facilities - "chemistry lab was like a kitchen sink", as you put it! I gather you don't have any clear ideas on what you might do yet - although I know you have kept a scrapbook of successful women across a variety of fields which, traditionally, have been dominated by men. I think you have the steely determination to do the same. The question that I know has been troubling you is - in what field?

I wonder if your final reports from your teachers across the subjects might hold a clue:

Miss Pleat (Needlework) - *"Amelia's skill is well established, but she refuses to follow the patterns. In the last class when we were all creating pinafores in which to do house work, she created a flying scarf. What use that will be to the subservient wife of a nice businessman, I'm really not sure"*.

Mr Ree (Science) - *"Amelia seems to blow hot and cold. On some aspects of science she leads the class, but on most she seems to be more interested in her own experiments with the aerodynamics of folded pieces of paper. My recommendation is she avoids any undertaking that is in the traditional fields of science or engineering"*.

Mr Fide (Geography) - "*I struggle to understand Amelia's thinking sometimes. She seems uninterested in understanding the fine-grained aspects of land, rocks and soil, while engrossed in mapping all aspects of the oceans (distances between islands etc.) - particularly the Atlantic (which is, well, basically empty). I simply fail to grasp what is driving her*".

Miss Peak (French) - "*Amelia is a wonderful student - and has really taken the classes seriously, as if she has her own motivational goals. She should go far*".

Perhaps I could suggest you do, after all, study what your teachers are saying - and perhaps listen to their observations (as opposed to some of their recommendations) as a guide to what you do next? Just trying to help.

All the best,

Timothy Shift

Targeted Delivery Date: September 1725

Sir Isaac Newton
Woolsthorpe-by-Colsterworth
Lincolnshire
England

My Dear Mr Newton,

Knowing that you have little time for small talk, let me commend you on your treatise Philosophiae Naturalis Principia Mathematica. An astounding body of work.

It is this work that instigated an idea in my mind that I hope you will find extremely interesting. However, when you learn from when and where I am writing this letter, your first instinct might be to shout "poppycock' and throw my missive away. I implore you not to do so.

You have postulated a set of laws pertaining to natural philosophy, in particular those concerning Time and Space. Paraphrasing, a body moves in a certain direction (space) and for a period (time) and this will not vary unless acted upon by another force.

The key point here is that I am writing this to you from the future. From 2046, in particular, but I assure you that time travel is not an abstract concept. There is an extreme reality attached to it. As tangible as being able to see, feel and touch other people you may meet. (Although, I have to be a bit more careful than you with that last element of 'touch' in this 'woke society' in which we now live).

Have you wondered just what Time and Space actually are? Well, here's a thought for you. I appreciate you are fully into your 82nd year, but were you, hypothetically speaking, to travel to Koenigsberg in Prussia and visit Johan and Anna Kant, they would delight in showing you their dear little boy, Immanuel. You could bounce him on your knee and tell him about your theories of Space and Time. He might remember your wise words for in later life he would himself declare:

> "Space and time are the pure (*a priori*) forms of sensible intuition. Intuition is contrasted with the conceptualization (or categorization) performed by the understanding, and involves the way in which we passively receive data through sensibility. Time is the pure (*a priori*) form of inner sense, i.e., our awareness of our own inner mental states."

I wonder if you might have mentioned that to him?

Should Mr Kant feel like getting out a little when in his 70's, he could travel to Brunswick in Germany to meet Carl F Gauss, a young man in his late twenties, who is a German mathematician and physicist who will come to make significant contributions to many fields in mathematics and science. I am sure they could have a splendid conversation over a beer as to the meaning of life and the reality of Time and Space. As real as the beer they are sharing.

In a similar vein, should Herr Gauss feel so inclined to share a beer or a plate of Haggis (I'd stick to the beer frankly) with James Clerk Maxwell in Scotland, he could congratulate Maxwell on his Classical theory of electromagnetic radiation.

Maxwell will need to get his skates on, but if he is brisk he will be able to go to Ulm in Wurttemburg, Germany to meet with Herman and Pauline Einstein. Anyway, I know the newborn child will be more interested in his next feed than Maxwell's laws on electromagnetic radiation but that's not the point. Maxwell was there. He could meet with Einstein in person. Einstein would be real. Einstein developed a relativistic interpretation of space and time which I absolutely know you would find fascinating and highly relevant to your own work.

And where am I going with all of this? You had an idea. There's no form or substance to an idea. It's just a notion. Certainly, the notions and principles developed from the idea go on to create certain material inventions but the ideas themselves have no corporal substance. You shaking hands with Kant would therefore be real as would his enjoying a beer with Gauss be real.

Einstein didn't especially want to meet with me although I was already five years old before he passed away. I guess I was more interested in my toys than space and time, again that's not the point. There would have been a reality to the meeting. A direct physical handshake or touch, all the way from you to me and then my reciprocating with this letter.

So what's the more real? Space and Time or my time-traveling letter? Careful with your answer. It's a trick question.

Yours sincerely,

Timothy Shift

p.s. How was the Apple Pie?

Targeted Delivery Date: August 1863

Charles Darwin
Down House, Bromley, Kent
England

Dear Mr Darwin,

I was wondering. While initially formulating the main thrust of your revolutionary ideas, did you viscerally feel the full scope of your premise, with the breadth and depth that we now come to associate with your 'On the Origin of Species'?

At the time of the initial publication of your work, there was considerable debate regarding Apes and Man. There is a commonality, if not a direct lineage, yet the scorn directed toward you by others was seemingly for the purpose of ridiculing the idea that Mankind too had evolved in a manner similar to animal species.

My question is this. At the time you first postulated your theory, had you backtracked the evolution of life all the way back to a few, single celled creatures, writhing in a primeval pond, or did you keep the basic animals of the world with their Phyla and Classes intact and just brought them along a few steps into their current form? Was there ever a point at which you suddenly thought, 'Good Heavens. We've all evolved from basically nothing to this state in which we find ourselves today.'? Did you ever think to yourself; 'I am perhaps one the few people in the entire world that realises that every living thing before us evolved from a basic single cell to be here today'? How did that make you feel? That's a profound idea that goes completely against every concept held by humankind up to that point.

I am aware that you shared your work with other close friends, so collectively, were you all in awe of the concept? Did you feel a strong schism developing between science and religion or were you subdued in this respect? Having spent so many years contemplating the publication of your ideas, perhaps you had completely come to terms with the whole thing.

I suppose you might be wondering where the thrust of my letter has been going? I assure you, I have no hidden agenda, no criticism and no preconception of your reply - just a hell of a lot of questions, as you have seen. I just want to understand what you felt about this sea change in the philosophy of where we all came from.

For any readers I have reproduced, below, the final words to be found in your own 'On the Origin of Species".

> "It is interesting to contemplate an entangled bank, clothed with many plants of many kinds, with birds singing on the bushes, with various insects flitting about, and with worms crawling through the damp earth, and to reflect that these elaborately constructed forms...have all been produced by laws acting around us....Thus, from the war of nature, from famine and death, the most exalted object which we are capable of conceiving, namely, the production of the higher animals directly follows....From so simple a beginning endless forms most beautiful and most wonderful have been, and are being, evolved."

I suppose it is just so typically in your DNA to have composed such a piece of prose to finish off your treatise. Don't worry if "….. in your DNA" doesn't resonate with you. It is a thoroughly relevant term, I assure you, and I'd gladly explain in a further letter. You've established the "What". I'm sure you'd be fascinated to hear about the "How".

Yours, most sincerely,

Timothy Shift

Targeted Delivery Date: December 1901

Professor Wilhelm Roentgen
University Of Munich
Bavaria
Weimar Republic

Dear Professor,

Let me congratulate you on recently being awarded the first ever Nobel Prize in Physics - for your discovery of a new kind of Ray. No, not the fish variety, but this strange new electromagnetic radiation that you called an "Unknown Ray" or "X-ray" for short (from the mathematical term 'X' for something that is unknown).

I gather that in fact your discovery in 1895 was actually by chance, as is so often the case - nothing to be ashamed about there. It's amazing what is found when you are just testing the basic apparatus - in your case, a light cover for the vacuum tube you were using....and there it was on the bench, a vague shimmer of green every time there was an electrical discharge. I so understand how you were consumed by the discovery, eating and sleeping in the lab for days to try and work out what was happening (and to make sure it was not a mistake!).

It must have been a shock when you first glimpsed an image of the bones in your hand when you accidentally placed it in front of the tube. I guess not as much as the shock your wife had when you *X-rayed* her hand. What was it she said upon seeing the image - "I have seen my death"? I always wondered if perhaps you cheekily did an X-ray of a hand shadow puppet (rabbit, or bird maybe) as the official image (rather than a flat hand), but then decided that the Royal Swedish Academy of Sciences might not see the joke.

Of course, like any new discovery it will take time to understand all the uses, as well as the risks, associated with it. That latter point, I fear, may take a while to appreciate fully. I gather that Nikola Tesla and Thomas Edison have raised some concerns, but hey, what do they know? There is a plan for all fine shoe shops up and down the land to install X-ray machines, so that little Jimmy's feet can be scanned every time he goes in there and he can get a giggle at seeing his bones. I mean, what could possibly go wrong?!

One final thing, and apologies if this sounds a bit morbid, but considering you are now a famous person, have you given any thought as to how you would want to be remembered? I don't know, maybe a clever inscription on a Tombstone? Or if that doesn't grab you, how about a chemical element being named after you?

Yours sincerely,

Timothy Shift

Targeted Delivery Date: January 1900

Gottlieb Daimler
Cannstatt
Kingdom of Württemberg
German Empire

Sehr geehrter Herr Daimler,

I have some information for you and also a complaint. But first, let me see if I have a correct understanding of how your automotive empire originated.

On your own, but often with your engineering partner Wilhelm Maybach, you were the technical originator of many firsts in the development of the small car engine. Your work on the Otto four stroke engine in 1876, the small, high-speed engines of 1882, the dream engine of 1833 all lead to the so called 1885 Grandfather clock engine, which culminated in the independent creation of your first automobile. I am well aware that a mere 60 miles down the road, a guy called Karl Benz also developed his motor car in 1885 but that was not a focus for you at this time. I understand your collaboration with Maybach bore fruit in 1889 with the launch of the first truly unique automobile, one that was not an adaptation of a horse-drawn carriage.

Then in 1890 you formed your own engine business, Daimler Motoren Gesellschaft (DMG). It is a common occurrence for visionary founders to be forced out of their own companies. But why oh why did you throw all your toys out of the pram and resign? So melodramatic and so unnecessary. At least you managed to buy your way back in with the help of the Englishman, Fredrick Simms, who invested £17,500 for the transfer of his shares to the British Daimler Company. In so doing, he obtained the rights to use the brand name Daimler for British Daimler Company products.

My complaint? Why on earth did you allow Jaguar to release Daimler limos. They did it right through the 60's? Why were some Jags called Daimlers and yet no Mercs were ever called Jaguar or Daimler? So confusing.

The big news? What you don't know is that in about 25 years, in 1926, your DMG company will merge with your old adversary, Karl Benz' company, Benz and Cie, to form Daimler-Benz based in Stuttgart. Karl Benz, the same man you fought in court in Mannheim in 1896 and to whom you had to pay royalties for several years. I really hope this little nugget of information of mine won't concern you. I don't normally go round spilling the beans, so I hope you don't get all upset. I know you've got a dicky heart and I don't want to cause you undue distress with this letter. However, I wanted to know why, after around 1900, the date that I calculate you will have received this letter, there are no more inventions or innovations credited as coming from you. Nothing, zero, Nix, Nicht. Was something concerning you......or........ Oh dear. Something else has just occurred to me, did something you read make you upset and unwell?

Mit freundlichem Gruß

Timothy Shift

Targeted Delivery Date: May 1871

Professor Emil Theodor von Wolff
University of Hohenheim
Bavaria
Germany

Dear Professor,

As an emerging scientist in the area of nutrition, I wanted to run an idea by you. I am sure you are intrigued, as are many, as to how the new role of the media might be able to shape public opinion and eating habits. I would like to propose an experiment.

You are, I believe, working on the second, expanded, edition of your analysis of the minerals and vitamin contents of various foods (by analysing the ash from burning the samples). It will be interesting to see, will it not, what effect your publication might have? I suggest, therefore, that you "by accident" introduce an error in one of the samples, purely in the interest of science, to determine if we can change the public's eating preferences. As luck would have it, there is an obvious candidate - that of spinach. In earlier texts by Moleschot and others, there is already some discrepancy in the iron content measured (perhaps some of the samples were contaminated?). So, all you would need to do is to summarise this earlier work in your results - let's choose something like, say, reporting 10 times the amount of iron that is actually present in spinach?

Imagine what could happen! Perhaps people will rush to eat (what they think is) this new super food? Governments might change policy for Farmers to enable them to grow more of these crops - a "new deal" they might call it. It might even become popularised in film or cartoons so that the message can get to the younger generation! Think of how we could prove the amplification impact of the media with this!

Now, I can guess what you are thinking - your scientific reputation is at stake - and I appreciate you do not want to tarnish this. That's the beauty of this idea, by referring to the earlier work (and picking a nice round factor like 10), you can subsequently defend yourself by pointing out the earlier errors and suggest that perhaps someone just put the decimal point in the wrong place. You know what conspiracy theorists are like - after much thought and deliberation, they'll even give it some catchy name like "the iron decimal point error". You'll be home free!

Yours sincerely,

Timothy Shift

p.s. What are film and cartoons? Don't give it too much thought, but keep an eye on a couple of brothers in Paris who go by the name of Lumière.

Targeted Delivery Date: March 1840

Mary Anning
Dorset
England

Dear Miss Anning,

A short letter from me, to both commend you as well as to point out something that I found very interesting. I believe that many people are now aware of your outstanding work discovering fossils on the 'Jurassic Coast' of Dorset. In my era it would be outrageously condescending for me to say this, but your endeavours are all the more astounding because you are a woman in the 1800s. You have become a notable authority on the fossilised remains of marine reptiles from the prehistoric period. At the tender age of twelve, while your friends where probably playing with their porcelain dolls, you went out and discovered the fossil of an Ichthyosaurs, followed by discoveries of both Plesiosaurus and Pterosaurs.

All amazing, but here's my specific reason to write to you. We all now know about dinosaurs and of course someone, even if not you, had to discover them to show they existed. What I didn't intuitively appreciate was that your discoveries also became a key piece of evidence for extinction.

I believe it was the Frenchman, Georges Cuvier, who had argued for the reality of extinction in the late 1790s based on his analysis of the fossils of mammals such as mammoths. Even so, I understand your contemporaries, many of who are scientifically literate people, still believe that just as new species did not appear, so existing species did not disappear — in part because they felt that extinction would thus imply that their creation had been imperfect. Any oddities found are being explained away as belonging to animals still living somewhere in an unexplored region of the Earth. I think they are starting to run out of places to look and, to be honest, if I said there has been something strange living at the bottom of my garden, it's much more likely to be a fox than an ichthyosaurs. That is, unless by some strange quirk of nature, ichthyosauri have developed a penchant for hard boiled eggs and saucers of milk, which is what I tend to leave out.

The ichthyosaurs, plesiosaurs, and pterosaur you found, show that during previous eras the Earth was inhabited by creatures quite different from those living today. An age when reptiles rather than mammals had been the dominant form of animal life. It is somewhat ironic that there's as much to glean from them no longer being here, as there is in the discovery that they used to be here.

One last point. You might be intrigued to hear that there's a refrain going around that refers to yourself, "She sells seashells by the seashore". Many people suggest you sang this while combing the beach for fossils. Unfortunately, without me being too specific, that song postdates you by over 50 years so if you were hoping to hear it for yourself - don't wait up.

Yours sincerely,

Timothy Shift

Targeted Delivery Date: May 1917

Glenn Curtiss
% Curtiss Aeroplane and Motor Company
Hammondsport
New York
United States of America

Dear Glen,

This letter reaches you, I suspect, at a difficult time for the USA, having just entered the First World War. The run up to this has been a real wake-up call for the military, who realised they were woefully short of aircraft of *any* type. The demand they made of your company last year was to come up with a 2-seater trainer aircraft - for which you designed the Curtiss JN-4, better known as the *Curtiss Jenny*. What an aircraft that turned out to be! Your company is now making them in their thousands (and not just for the USA - it is successful worldwide). The Navy is pleased as punch as well, as another of your aircraft has demonstrated the first take-off and landing from a ship. I don't think anyone uttered the words Top Gun at the time, but you have to start somewhere.

Of course, designs like this don't come out of the blue. You are one of the most successful aeronautical engineers in history. I wonder if you ever thought things would turn out this way when you were racing around as a Western Union bicycle messenger, and then developing your own single-cylinder motorcycles, winning races and breaking records left, right, and centre. I love the design of your first carburettor, btw, made out of a soup can! And you repeated the same feats with your early aircraft - speed records and prizes galore.

In fact, you and the Wright brothers were neck-and-neck in the early days, and were serious rivals. Maybe Wilbur didn't like it that the Aero Club of America issued you with Pilot's Licence #1 (while he only got #5)? But then it was done alphabetically! I know you blamed him for the death of one of your friends in a crash of one of their aircraft. It also didn't help that they were suing you, I suspect. You weren't alone in being sued - and many think that this patent war is seriously stifling the aircraft industry. Maybe you felt something had to be done to try and clip their wings. However, your approach was, I have to say, somewhat underhand. In conjunction with the head of the Smithsonian Institute, secretly modifying one of Samuel Langley's earlier (failed) aircraft to prove it could actually fly, and then taking out the modifications before it went on display, seems going beyond the pale. The result is that the current head of the Smithsonian (Charles Walcott) has now declared Samual Langley (who just happens to be a previous head of the Smithsonian) as the person who invented the first heavier-than-air flying machine capable of flight, instead of the Wright brothers. Blimey! Maybe you and Charles feel you have got away with this, but I have to remind you that, nearly always, the truth will out.

I don't know if you realise it, but you are a dad many times over. Forgive me, I am not trying to cast any aspersions on your marital status, but as well as fathering two sons with your wife, Lena, you have also been called the Father of the Aviation Industry and the Father of Naval Aviation. The reality is that the Wright brothers may have achieved the first flight and developed the principles of steering and control (sorry, it's true, there, I've said it), but you made aircraft commercially successful. In fact, you never know - things may well come full circle, since I am sure there would be advantages to your company and the Wright Aeronautical Corporation working together to capitalise on the emerging aircraft market. I appreciate that things might seem too raw right now, but I wouldn't rule it out.

Actually, of all the inventions you worked on, it is the flying car that I had questions about. Building a flying car is a tough gig - we are still tinkering with that today. Although technically we can make it work, building them economically for the masses is still a pipe dream. Your first attempt this year (1917) of the *Curtiss Autoplane* did manage a few hops and was exhibited at the Pan-American Aeronautical Exposition. It wasn't quite, "cut a Ford model T and one of our trainer aircraft in half and bolt them together", but probably not far off! However, there are a couple of potential aspects about which I do have concerns. Do you really need the extra lift you are trying to generate with those smaller, colourful side wings that fold out from under the car? Second, pay attention to the engine and exhaust systems to ensure maximum efficiency - any roughness in running can cause problems. For instance, noises like gritty-gritty-pop-pop would be particularly worrisome.

Yours sincerely,

Timothy Shift

p.s. "btw" - sorry, that stands for "by the way", it is hard not to let text-speak slip into my writings. What's text-speak? Well, oh… actually…never mind…don't worry about that for now.

Targeted Delivery Date: 22 March 1973

Werner Heisenberg
% Harvard University
Cambridge
Massachusetts
United States of America

Dear Herr Heisenberg,

I'm having a devil of a job trying to get in touch with you.

I understood that from late 1955, you would be in Scotland at St Andrews University. Unfortunately, I didn't exactly know that you would be giving the Gifford Lectures on the intellectual history of physics. The university staff suggested you may just be teaching and so were most unhelpful and I missed you there.

Subsequently in 1957, I thought I knew precisely what you were involved with since you were a signatory of the Göttinger Manifest. At the risk of being corrected, I understand you were taking a public stand against the Federal Republic of Germany arming itself with nuclear weapons. Accordingly, I wrote to you at the Max-Planck-Institut für Physik but I didn't quite understand that it had been moved to Munich. I believe the Institute was expanded and renamed. I appreciate I should have been more precise. I now know it was called the Max-Planck-Institut für Physik und Astrophysik (MPIFA). That's an awfully similar name but unfortunately the staff at your old location wanted a far more accurate address from me, and yet again didn't pass the letter on to you.

As recently as 1973, I knew exactly that you were to give a lecture at Harvard University on the historical development of the concepts of quantum theory, so I wrote to you a third time there. This time the letter just didn't get to you in time because I hadn't realised how tight your schedule was, and that on 24 March 1973 you were to give a speech before the Catholic Academy of Bavaria, accepting the Romano Guardini Prize. The "Scientific and Religious Truth", I believe.

I really haven't been successful reaching you at all. It would appear I either knew what you were doing or where you were, but regretfully, never both pieces of information at the same time.

You seem to have an aura of uncertainty about you that seems to be almost one of the principle laws of physics. I'll send this letter again to the Plank Institute and see what happens.

Yours sincerely,

Timothy Shift

Targeted Delivery Date: October 1923

Marie Curie
℅ The Radium Institute
Paris
France

Dear Marie,

As you are currently writing the biography of your late husband, Pierre, I thought I might just let you know one of the things that I find most inspiring about you. Yes, you were the first woman to win a Nobel Prize (jointly with your husband), the first (and to date only) woman to win two Nobel Prizes (in different disciplines as well - the first in Physics, the second in Chemistry). Furthermore, you led the Radium Institute, uncovering the core facets of radioactive elements, such as Radium and Polonium, as well as detailing how radiation will kill tumour cells faster than healthy cells (leading to many modern cancer treatments). Even your daughter and son-in-law will be awarded Nobel Prizes as they expand on your work. Amazing achievements, without a doubt.

However, what I really love is the way you responded to a reporter's question following that Nobel Prize awarded to both you and your husband in 1903. When you were asked "what does it feel like to be married to a genius", you replied "I haven't a clue, you should ask my husband". Classic.

Yours sincerely,

Timothy Shift

Target Delivery Date: June 1860

Michael Faraday
Hampton Court
London
England

Dear Mr Faraday,

I'm in a quandary and am turning to you for some advice. You see, I'm from the future, which is not wholly germane to my question, so please take it at face value for the moment. A quick question about your Faraday cage. As I understand it, if you construct a box with all six sides of a conductive material, then there should be no electromagnetic fields inside. Am I correct?

That being the case, if I happen to be on a mobile phone call when I enter the lift to get to my apartment, once those doors close, shouldn't I lose the signal completely? Why doesn't the line drop? I can continue to talk quite happily.

Well, when I say quite happily, that's incorrect. Actually, I'm not happy at all. Since the phone is working, I must assume that there has been some extreme cost-cutting going on, and that my safe-as-houses lift is not made of metal after all but of wood or plastic or some-such recyclable nonsense. Now I don't know about you, but I like to be surrounded by thick gauge steel when I'm in a small box being hauled several hundred feet up into the air.

Frankly, I think the cost-cutting I'm uncovering is more conspiratorial than sound economics. I've started to see traces of it everywhere. The bathrooms were meant to be built using Carrara marble but they all seem to have Corian worktops everywhere. There were meant to be the finest Wilton wool carpets in the corridors, but everyone can see they've installed polyester, commercial grade carpeting.

Oh, modern living! It's full of first world problems; lifts; mobile phones; dropped phone lines; plastic; Corian and polyester etc. I suddenly see now I've been taken for a ride here by the building contractors. The lift is the tip of the iceberg - I don't care about it right now. I'm going to sue the contractors for fraud.

I'll have to write again and explain all my strange words and phrases. Also, don't worry about my mentioning time travel either. I've had enough. Frankly, I'd rather be back in your time when you could hire a reputable builder like nice Mr Jerry of Jerry Bros of Liverpool. You knew where you were with a Jerry-built house.

Yours sincerely,

Timothy Shift

Targeted Delivery Date: March 1630

Galileo Galilei
Pisa
The Duchy of Florence

Dear Galileo Galilei,

I wanted to write to just let you know that the mistake you made by inadvertently going to that geometry lecture, while studying medicine at the University of Pisa, turned out for the good. Ok, I know the pay for a mathematician is less than that of a medical doctor, but some of the stuff you then worked on has had quite an impact!

I am pleased you enjoyed the views from Pisa so much - and dropping those different balls off the side was an inspired idea (I don't care what they say, I know who did it). These days we play Pooh-sticks instead, but you'll have to wait awhile to get that reference. By the way, I agree with you, it seems crazy that heavy things don't intrinsically fall faster than light ones - you were spot on. That Aristotle guy was smart for his time, but every dog has his day, right? And it's a good thing you spotted that the moon wasn't just a translucent perfect disc..... since we actually landed some people on it a few decades ago. One of them dropped a hammer and a feather at the same time and watched them hit the surface together, since there was no air resistance. You would have loved it!

We call the moon Earth's satellite, by the way. The same as those satellites you spotted around Jupiter in a nice orbit. I know Saturn was confusing for you - who would have thought a planet could have rings! Talking of satellites, this message may get to you through one of the many artificial satellites we have put into orbit around the earth. How did we do that? Ah, well.... So, you know those calculations you made about how objects should fall along a parabola? (The army loved that, btw, it made targeting the enemy easier!). As you know the faster you fire a cannon ball, the further it goes, but still falling to earth. Now, imagine you were sitting in Florence, and you fired a ball faster and faster. What would happen? Ok, I know, yes, you would hit the Duomo....and you don't want to annoy your friend Cosmo II of the Medici family any more than you have to (you are going to have enough problems with Popes as it is). So, assuming you can miss the church, and you continued to increase the speed of the ball, and the parabola got longer and longer....in the end the ball would be falling along exactly the same curvature of the earth, and (except for air resistance) it would keep "falling" round the earth for ever! Well, that's how we launch satellites, just with a much bigger cannon. Neat, eh?

Anyway, I'd better go - I'm actually feeling a bit under the weather, so my wife is going to take my temperature with a thermometer to make sure I'm not running a fever. Yes, that invention of yours worked out too!

All the best, and remember, if you get any whiff of an inquisition, perhaps yelling "The truth? You can't handle the truth!" at the top of your voice, may be a little excessive. Try to just mutter the truth under your breath.

Timothy Shift

p.s. I know you don't put a lot of credence in the fact that there are two high tides (rather than one) every day in Venice - but I do think this might be significant. Try and check it out, and think about whether that might affect your ideas that the tides are just caused by the seas sloshing about due to the motion of the earth.

Retail & Commerce

Targeted Delivery Date: February 1492

Christopher Columbus
Valladolid
Castille
Crown of Castile

Dear Chris,

Congratulations on getting your start-up funded! I know how hard it is to close a first investment round like that - it's like herding cats, right? And those Angel investors are such prima donnas. It's like they think they are royalty or something! Oh, I see...I guess in your case they really are. It's also amazing how some people just don't have the vision. Kings of Portugal and England struggle with seeing the big picture. Smart move of yours to wait until all that fighting by Ferdinand and Isabella had finished before making your final pitch - timing is everything in these situations. And you have got to know when to step back from the table as well - so pretending to go off and look for other backers made them even more hungry. Great that you closed the investment from Queen Isabella - nice to see girl power is alive and well in the fifteenth century!

I've been looking through your business plan - and actually I do have a few questions/comments:

1) So, as I understand it, the plan is to sail west (rather than east) in order to find a quicker route to Asia - saves having to sail round Africa...which would be a real boon. That Cape of Storms, as named by Bartolomeu Dias (a Portuguese peer of yours, do you know him?), is a real challenge isn't it? No wonder they changed its name to Cape of Good Hope to make people less scared. That's a bit like an old Viking called Erik naming a place Greenland! However, assuming your plan works, I presume your unique selling point (USP) would be a

reduction in shipping costs and timing for those valuable goods? Time is money, as they say - but I do have some concerns about your projections for the length of the voyage - 2,300 miles seems pretty short. I know this is based on your estimate of the circumference of the earth (and you, and most of your colleagues, already know the earth is round - none of this flat earth nonsense). However, I'd advise you to read up on that guy Eratosthenes (276-194 BC) - since his estimates seem reasonably sound and are at least 3x that of yours.

2) I am a bit worried about how you stop other competitors getting in on the action - i.e., won't the route quickly become public knowledge? I see that you plan to have all the sailors sign Non-Disclosure Agreements (NDAs) to protect your Intellectual property (IP). However, I see a couple of flaws in that approach. First, at least in England, most fifteenth century sailors tend to be illiterate and struggle even giving a thumb print (it's a scandal, I know, the adult education departments in our local authorities really need to up their game). Second, and again maybe it is different in Italy and Spain, but here in England if you take a random sailor down The Dog & Duck, ply him with a few pints of the landlord's finest ale, mention the word florin a couple times, they'll tell you whatever you want to know.

3) The term sheet for your investment is a bit unusual. I like the fact that you get a 10% cut on all the merchandise, and you get first option on buying into follow-on commercialisation at a discount, but what's this about you getting to be governor and overlord of new lands? I just wonder if that might be a bit distracting? Building communities is a specialist skill and very different to that of an entrepreneurial risk-taker. How broad is your leadership team? Do you have these roles covered? I'd recommend making sure your team is as diverse as possible - don't make that old mistake of keeping it in the family - it can lead to disaster. I know you want to be bold, but keep that cautious edge too - you don't want to be so far out in front that

you are like the cowboy getting arrows in his back (hmm, maybe that analogy won't make sense to you yet, it's a bit "cart before the horse").

So, I wish you well as you prepare to launch v1.0 of your solution - your first voyage west on the Santa Maria. Remember that most start-ups usually end up doing something different to what was initially planned - it depends on what they find with that 1.0 product. So, keep an open mind as to what you find out there - it may be different from what you expect.

All the best,

Timothy Shift

p.s. Oh and try to make sure you are seen as the first. If you happen to come across any Viking artefacts, I'd keep that quiet...no point in scaring the investors unnecessarily.

Targeted Delivery Date: October 1878

John Harvey Kellogg
% Battle Creek Sanatorium
Battle Creek
Michigan
United States of America

Dear John,

It's funny how things pan out, isn't it? Through your sterling work at the Sanatorium on better health and eating, you are changing the way people start their day. Before you, the typical breakfast diet in America was a myriad of meats, fritters, pastries, pies etc., leading to a national emergency in terms of indigestion.

Your goal for more bland foods is being realised through your chance discovery (with your brother Will and others) of how to create flakes of wheat or corn by leaving some rolled dough out overnight, and then roasting them in the morning. What an invention - Corn Flakes! While starting your day with a bowl of your new flakes may well alleviate the indigestion epidemic, I am less sure that it will cure "unnatural sexual desire" as you are claiming. Well, not if the contents of various dubious websites containing the words *morning* and *quickie* are anything to go by.

While I am sure that you will be pleased that your goal to change what people eat for breakfast across the population is being realised, I am personally just glad some of your other recommended procedures from the Sanatorium have not also become common practice. For instance, creating a healthy gut with regular enemas as you have been experimenting with (first with water, then with yogurt). Did your patients really go for this? While this might do wonders for one's gut bacteria, to be honest getting three kids to eat their Rice Krispies for breakfast and getting them ready for school is hard enough, without having to do *that* to them all. I mean, think of the mess all over the kitchen.

Yours sincerely,

Timothy Shift

Targeted Delivery Date: August 1810

Mary Ann Brailsford
75 Church Street
Southwell
Nottinghamshire
England

Dear Mary,

Congratulations on completing your science project! Usually, kids build models or do drawings to illustrate their chosen subject. You, however, were determined to let nature show off your selected topic. So, last year you decided to plant some apple pips in the garden (I think you took them from the apples your mother was using to make a pie). Hopefully, by now, you can see your sapling growing, demonstrating your project has been a success. Full marks!

You might wonder why this strange bloke from the future is writing to you about apples and your science project. Well, that's because your apple tree will become famous. I know that sounds ludicrous, and your hand is already hovering over the rubbish bin with this letter. However, I assure you it is true. It turns out that your little sapling will start bearing fruit in a few years, and that fruit turns out to be rather delicious in pies. So nice, in fact, that people ask for cuttings, and then plant offspring of your little tree. Although your family may not own the cottage by then, the new owner (by the name of Matthew Bramley), encourages this - but insists that all the trees bear his name. And so, the Bramley Apple is born. So why does this make your apple tree special, I hear you ask? After all, yours wasn't the 'first' apple tree of this type. What about the trees that produced the apples that you took the pips from? Well, it turns out that none of those other trees survived. Only yours, and all the cuttings taken from it, made it. So, every single one of the approximately 6 billion Bramleys sold each year in my time are descended from your tree and that one pip you planted. Wow, what do you think of that? I suspect you are thinking, "who the hell is eating all those Apples?", given the population of England in 1810 is only 10 million. Well, population growth is a long story - and probably best saved for another letter.

I heard a rumour that you have a new science project this year, for which you hope to plant additional crops around your apple tree. I believe you are thinking of blackberries, some orchids (genus: vanilla), micro wheat (good for pastry, I gather), and if understood correctly, a custard bush? Hmm, you may want to get your cookery and biology teachers together to talk that one through. However, I like your thinking - whole dish planting! You never know, that really might catch on.

Finally, you may be amazed to hear that your apple tree is still alive and bearing fruit more than 200 years after you planted it - and it is now known as the 'mother' of the Bramley Apple. Unfortunately, I do have to let you know that sadly, given the age of the tree, it is now suffering from a type of fungal infection which means she has seen better days. However, I think she is still rooting for you, and remembers all the care and attention you gave her.

Best of luck in your ongoing studies.

Yours sincerely,

Timothy Shift

Targeted Delivery Date: January 1887

John Stith Pemberton
Pemberton House
11 7th Street,
Columbus
Georgia
United States of America

Dear John,

A Happy New Year to you! I hope you are doing OK health-wise
now, since I know you have been a bit in the wars (literally). That
sabre wound to the chest you sustained at the Battle of Columbus
in 1865 was nasty, and treatment on the battlefield was, well,
somewhat primitive - but at least they had strong pain relief.
However, this turned out to be both a blessing and a curse, since
you became addicted to morphine, like so many others returning
from the war.

As a biochemist and pharmacist, I guess it was natural for you to
work on possible substitutes for morphine to aid not just yourself,
but an increasingly concerned public regarding drug addiction. It's
strange really - today we tend to think of such addictions as a
modern phenomenon, but of course that's far from the truth. Your
experiments with various toxic plants eventually led you to mix
cocaine with some of the existing cocaine-laced wines (such as the
French *Vin Mariani*), some caffeine (from kola nuts) as well as a
few other ingredients, including damiana (believed to be an
aphrodisiac) - and *Pemberton's French Wine Coca* was born!
Although you had planned this to be aimed at war veterans, its use
spread. It was interesting how you marketed it as being beneficial to
"ladies, and all those whose sedentary employment causes nervous
prostration". As an aside, I'm not sure how to break this to you, but
replacing morphine with cocaine is unlikely to cure the national

drug addiction problem.

Just when things were going great - what happens? The temperance movement! Now, never let it be said that any problem was too much for a Pemberton, so you set about adapting your French Wine Coca into a non-alcoholic variety. Let's gloss over the fact that the temperance rules had no issue with whatever amount of cocaine you cared to include - but alcohol, well, that was a no-no. In reformulating the drink to remove the wine, one of those chance mistakes happened that would change things for ever - you mistakenly mixed in carbonated water. And voilà! You had a your new "temperance-approved" health drink ready for soda fountains, which you decided to market as a "valuable brain tonic" among other things. That was a cute name that Frank Robinson (your adverting guru) came up with: *Coca-Cola* - it says what's in the tin (btw, have you ever thought about using bottles?). Of course, I guess technically it should have been called *Coca-Kola*, however Frank believed that writing it with two Cs would have a better marketing impact. [As an aside, if he has time, could you ask Frank to drop a line to a certain Coco Channel in Saumur, France to let her in on his thinking - could be useful to her in the future]. Frank even wrote out the Coca-Cola name in some weird curly script - I guess he knows what he is doing. I hope you are not too disappointed in selling, on average, only 9 drinks a day in the first year?

In fact, going forward, I'd spend more time with Frank...he may be on to something. I have read that you are going to advertise the new drink as exhilarating, invigorating, pure joy, refreshing...and some other word I can't read in your papers - since I think someone has actually spilt Coca-Cola on it and stained it...I think the word is something like lipsmacking-thirstquenchin'-ace-tastin'.....no, sorry can't read the rest. Maybe it's nothing. Forget I mentioned it - perhaps such a made-up phrase might not be right for you anyway.

Finally, I know there are those sniffing around looking to buy you out. Difficult decision I know, especially if you want to secure some future for you and your son (and I know your health does still worry you). I think there is an offer in the air for something of the order of $1,500 all in? If you do decide to sell, I'd really try and push them up (even if it's only a bit) - feels like they would be getting it for a song to me.

Yours sincerely,

Timothy Shift

---------- Letter from Timothy Shift Esq. ----------

Targeted Delivery Date: September 1903

Mary ("Stagecoach") Fields
Great Falls
Montana
United States of America

Dear Mary,

I am raising a glass and writing to congratulate you on your retirement, at the age of 71, from being a US Postal Service Star Route Carrier, delivering mail from Cascade, Montana to the St. Peter's Mission.

I don't know if you realised, but when you won the contract for this route in 1895, this made you the first ever African American female to carry mail for the post office! My understanding is that your service has been exemplary, you never missed a day's work in all that time. I suspect your work ethic was formed from your earlier time at the mission, where you undertook many of the maintenance duties traditionally carried out by men. I am sure there must have been a reasonable explanation for the fact that you often got into gun duels with some of the hired male help. History doesn't record the outcome of these duels, but then again, you are still here and they are not!

As part of your mail route you had to contend with attacks by bandits and wolves, and you carried a number of firearms (including a Smith & Wesson under your apron). In contrast, the main worry for my postie is the chihuahua at No. 36. I can only imagine the challenges of the weather there in a typical Montana winter. I gather deep snow often prevented the stagecoach and horses from getting through, so you would continue on foot so as not to miss the mail train. I must check the current postal workers' terms and conditions, but I'm pretty sure "delivery on foot in snowstorm with

5-foot drifts" won't be a standard part of the job specification.

From you having been born enslaved in Tennessee, to becoming a respected and much-loved figure in Cascade, you are now an inspiration to many. I wish you a happy retirement - and am delighted to hear that the special dispensation for you to be allowed to drink liquor in the saloon with the menfolk will continue. I just hope they are ready for you!

Yours sincerely,

Timothy Shift

Targeted Delivery Date: January 1269

Marco Polo
The House of Niccolò Polo
Venice
Republic of Venice

Dear Milione,

Tickets. Boarding cards. Foreign Money. Since you are such an experienced traveller, you know the drill but I do so hope this reaches you before you depart on your trip to China with your dad and uncle. I also hope you don't mind me using your nickname - it seems so appropriate. I gather you are planning to document your journey, along with what you discover, and publish this in some kind of travel guide. I hear you plan to call it something like "Rough Guide to the Silk Route". Snappy! I like it.

I have reviewed your planned itinerary, which I must say is very impressive. If I have a concern, it is that you might be aiming a bit high for the average traveller. For example:

- Some of your accommodation appears to be in the palace of Kublia Kan (1st Emperor of the Yuan dynasty), along with an audience with the emperor himself. While I am all for inspiring travellers, I don't quite see how this would scale. Is the emperor OK with package holidays in groups of 200 meeting with him and staying over? Would meals, lodging, and entertainment be provided? What is the connectivity situation there? It sounds kind of remote.

- Some of the excursions you plan consist of undertaking diplomatic missions on the emperor's behalf, across Indonesia, Burma, Sri Lanka and other parts of his empire. While I think selling this in the form of corporate team building events, where guests have to role play, is an interesting idea, I do worry about the liability insurance requirements to cover all eventualities. I mean, you wouldn't want anyone starting a war or anything.

- Although I appreciate that the timing of your return trip is somewhat up in the air, I think I must be mistaken that it is possible the whole trip might take around 24 years? While there is a market for longer travel for sabbaticals etc., the average time most people can get off work is around 2 weeks. Is there a possibility that you could document an expedited tour as an option? I do appreciate that getting round the standard sailing time of at least 4 months might be problematic, so I am interested in how you plan to handle this in your guide so as to appeal to the widest audience.

Finally, I would advise keeping a lookout for any unusually large structures, such as boundary walls. Things like that can be featured in a travel guide and show an authentic touch and provide confirmation that you know the locale well. It would seem odd if something really significant was omitted.

All the best for your trip,

Timothy Shift

Targeted Delivery Date: November 1585

Isaac Le Maire
Amsterdam
Holland

Dear Issac,

I hope you are settling in well in Amsterdam, after your move from Antwerp. Never a great thing to have to relocate in a hurry - but then I guess you didn't have much choice as the city was being ransacked by the Spanish. Tough to make sure you grab all the essentials you need in these kinds of situations, and I'm not sure how many of your 22 children were with you at the time, but hopefully they all got out as well.

I have to admit I am writing this slightly under the influence of alcohol - a very fine French Brandy, to be exact. Actually, Brandy is the subject of this letter. I am trying to locate (and congratulate) the 16th century Dutch shipmaster who first came up with the cunning plan of simplifying the shipping of wine by distilling it down to a concentrate, and then adding water again at the other end before drinking it. Given that you are a merchant of some repute, I wonder if you know who the shipmaster was - could it even be yourself? A clever way of cutting your shipping costs! But things didn't turn out as planned. Some wise-crack decided to try drinking the liquid neat, and discovered that it tasted rather good! In fact, far better than the wine from which it was distilled.

However nice it tasted, it was pretty potent stuff, and hence one needed some way of measuring *how* potent. You are living in the burgeoning Golden Age, and want to have a good time out on the town drinking it, but without waking up in the morgue. I gather there were several methods attempted to measure the concentration. My favourite is the one where you soak gunpowder with it, then see if it will explode on lighting it, after burning off the alcohol! I mean, what could possibly go wrong? That's probably the other way of ending up in the morgue. It was a bit of a crude measure of course - and it could only prove if the concentration was above a certain point (which became known as the "proof", as in "to test if a thing is true", something we still us today). Leading also, of course, to the word Brandy itself, which comes from the Dutch word *Brandewijn*, meaning "burnt wine".

Oh, and the reason I wanted to get in touch with the person who came up with this clever approach to re-constituting wine? Well, I think they are missing a trick. Given the likely global reach of their trade routes, I was thinking that they could turn their hand to other food stuffs in concentrate. For example, imagine bringing in some produce from the Far East, removing any liquid and then selling it in some kind of container or pot, ready for re-constitution by adding hot water. I don't know, something like noodles maybe? I think you could make a killing.

Yours sincerely,

Timothy Shift

Targeted Delivery Date: June 2016 (but hey, who cares, time just passes when you're out on the water)

Jack O'Neill
Ocean Highway 1
San Francisco
United States of America

Hey Jack,

I just wanted to say what a splendid job you have done in building the O'Neill sportswear company on the back of your own focussed needs. The wetsuit you designed, to meet your own requirements, allows one to surf for much longer in the cold waters of the Pacific Ocean, on the Northern California coastline. Your company wetsuit strap-line, "It's always summer on the inside", really does sum it up.

It's become a bit of a stereotypical story for Californian businesses. In 1952, you founded the O'Neill brand while opening one of California's first surf shops in a garage on the Great Highway in San Francisco. Of course it would have to be in a garage, WeWork hadn't established rental start-up offices back then. There must be building-design companies in California who do nothing else other than fit-out a garage to be suitable for starting a business. HP and Apple to name but two that started that way.

Strangely, although you are widely credited as the inventor of the wetsuit, an investigation concluded that UC Berkeley physicist Hugh Bradner was perhaps more likely to have been the original inventor. I really don't think that anyone cares because physicists are always inventing loads of stuff that they never commercialise. It needs a strong character like you, patch over one eye, an ex-navy pilot running a big sportswear company. Hugh Bradner may have dabbled with neoprene back in the lab, but you're the guy donning the suit and heading out in the cold breaks in the Pacific. You get my vote any day.

I'll tell you who's also pleased with what you've done. The bars and cafes up and down the California coastline who like to see you guys at sundown. Come in and have a few beers, tell a few stories and spend a little money. You can't do that if you're covered in goose fat. No, the goose fat guys are heading home for a good scrape and several showers. And the smell? You don't want them in your bar or cafe. All that wiping down of tables and chairs, glasses smashing as they fail to hold them in their greasy hands, the increased public liability insurance for people slipping and breaking limbs. No sir.

Anyway, I hope you carry on taking the drop around Mavericks and don't mind getting letters from a Hodad like me.

Cowabunga dude,

Timothy Shift

Targeted Delivery Date: April 1770

The Right Honourable John Montagu
The 4th Earl of Sandwich
Hinchingbrooke House
Huntingdonshire
England

My Lord,

I want to pass on my hearty congratulations for your many fine achievements, including First Lord of The Admiralty and Postmaster General, to name but two. However, you may be chagrined to hear that for all your achievements in these high offices of state, it is your creation of the humble sandwich for which you are most remembered (or "meat between two slices of bread" as you so eloquently first called it).

I gather that the inspiration came from the desire to satisfy your hunger whilst being able to continue playing at cards/gambling - and hence the key prerequisite of not requiring any cutlery. It seems the sandwich fit the bill perfectly. However, I'm not sure it has totally solved the problem since most of your gambling equipment, which has been handed down and is now considered a family heirloom, is still covered in copious quantities of goose fat, gravy and other animal oils - to the point that they are still considered a danger to public health to this day.

That aside, I think you are definitely onto something with this invention - and I gather you plan to commercialise the making of these sandwiches on an industrial scale. To that end, I am somewhat concerned over some the filling/naming you are planning, for example:

- Your signature sandwich - the *BLT* (Beaver, Lettuce and

Tomato). Great abbreviation, by the way, easy to remember and quick to order! Now, I know that beaver tail is a popular delicacy in the 18th century (due to the fact that beaver tail is considered, essentially, a fish since it is slightly scaly and spends much of its time in water), but I do wonder if this could really be expanded successfully to the masses? Maybe try a substitute that is more commonly available?

- The *Enthronement Chicken* sandwich sounds very regal and a nice nod to the new King (George III). However, I'm not sure the name really rolls off the tongue...maybe play around with that one.

- Your simple *Blacksmiths* sandwich of cheese and pickle sounds delicious - although I do wonder if you might consider whether there are other trades that might be more in need? Perhaps those that are not so close to home - for example, workers in the fields?

This new endeavour could really revolutionise what people eat for luncheon. Have you thought about upselling other items with the sandwich? For example, I can imagine you offering a great deal for a meal on, say, a BLT, a packet of wild boar scratchings and a yard of diet Ale.

One final thing, I wonder if you have considered a partner to aid expansion? I'd recommend you try and track down the ancestors of a couple of likely lads by the names of Michael Marks and Tom Spencer, and talk through your ideas.

All the best,

Timothy Shift

Targeted Delivery Date: Aug 1974

Robert P. McCulloch
% Thunderbird Country Club
Palm Springs
California
United States of America

Dear Bob,

It is not often I get to write to someone who has had such a varied career. It seems to me that your early working years in California and Wisconsin, during the 1930s and 1940s, were all about engines. It didn't matter what they powered - airplane, boat, lawnmower - if it ran off gasoline and made a nice noise, you were all over it. Maybe this was your ancestry showing through, given that your grandfather was a prolific implementor of a number of the electrical and power inventions of Thomas Edison.

While a number of your contemporaries were perhaps ahead of you in some of the markets, for example Briggs & Stratton for lawnmowers and Ralph Evenrude in boats, you spotted a new niche opportunity for your engines. Chainsaws! Now, I'm not really sure why you thought that arming every redneck around with an engine on a stick connected to a chain was a good idea, but you rapidly built a business out of it. Trees were felled at a prodigious rate, almost as fast as the hospitals could treat the self-inflicted wounds. As an aside, did you ever go wandering through the woods, your trusted McCulloch 3-25 in hand, and say to yourself "You know, I feel like a lumberjack, and I'm alright" (or words to that effect)? I just had to ask. You will be pleased to hear that your chainsaws are still in use today, sold under the *Husqvarna* brand.

What to do with all the wealth that your growing business was generating? I suspect most people would just stash it away - but not you. As well as starting a car business (*Paxton Automotive*) which built a car, along with components like superchargers for the industry, you had much bigger plans - to build a city! So in 1963 you made the largest ever land purchase in Arizona of some 26 square miles in a place called Lake Havasu, whose only claim to fame to date had been the location of a World War II army base. As well as building several manufacturing plants to churn out more chainsaws, you started to lay out the city itself. Sure, you had nice wide streets, malls, schools etc. - but you wanted something to make your city famous. So, you settled on a bridge over the river that divided the newly minted Lake Havasu City. Rather than build it, you decided to buy one! One of ours, actually - London Bridge to be precise, for around $2.4m. You had it broken down into blocks, shipped around the world to California and then trucked to Arizona where it was rebuilt. What a fantastic grand opening that was in 1971, with dignitaries galore. Even the Mayor of London came along - mainly, I suspect, because he refused to believe such a ridiculous escapade unless he saw it with his own eyes. Today, the bridge holds the world record of being the largest antique, presumably because it is still classified as being a mobile object! I don't know if you were amused or annoyed to hear the urban myth grow up that you actually bought the wrong bridge, and had intended to buy Tower Bridge. While this made a great story, we both know that this simply wasn't true.

Even with the bridge, you weren't done. In the last few years you have built your first airplane, a kind of blend of airplane and helicopter, and are busy testing it. As ever, you are dreaming big - and plan to market it so you can enable an "airplane in every garage in America". I have to warn you, that's a tough gig. For reference, there's the guy called Steve over in what has recently become known as Silicon Valley, who is mulling on starting a company that will attempt to put a computer into every home in America. This is going to take the best part of thirty years, so good luck with the airplane idea.

Finally, I don't know which of the various aspects of your career you are most proud? While it is probably your technical achievements, it may also be that you always had time to act the prankster with your grandchildren. Well, I'll let you into a secret that it is for that bridge you will be most remembered. What an inspired and audacious idea! But then again, who knew that the man who bought London Bridge also invented the chainsaw?

Yours sincerely,

Timothy Shift

Targeted Delivery Date: October 1925

William J. A. Bailey
The Bailey Radium Laboratories
East Orange
New Jersey
United States of America

Dear William,

I am writing to express my concern regarding your range of radium enhanced products, particularly your classic line of Radithor (certified Radioactive Water). I know that you see this as an all-curing elixir drink, and I gather your marketing slogan is "A Cure for the Living Dead". I suspect, unfortunately, that only half of that statement will turn out to be true. Also, I don't seem to see Oil of Snake listed in the ingredients, I wonder if it was somehow missed off?

I know that this is the latest in a line of radium-enhanced products like, for example, your earlier Arium tablets, designed to give a man a boost, err, in the bedroom department, or "Super-Man Power" (as you so delicately put it). My concern comes from the fact that I am unsure how much long-term testing you have done on these products. I mean, feeling perky for a while is all well and good, but what of the prolonged affects? Your good friend and distributor Eben Byers is drinking this stuff like it is going out of fashion (as well as selling a significant amount based on his Golf celebrity status). I gather while he says he is feeling well, he does have a lot of pains in his jaw and teeth, which perhaps should be investigated.

Of course, I appreciate that other companies are trying to steal a march on you - particularly the German company Auergesellschaft, with their Radioactive toothpaste. You must admit their slogan is not bad either: "Your teeth will shine with radioactive brilliance".

Who wouldn't want that?

Overall, I would urge caution - that new Food & Drug Administration seems to look interested in what you are doing.

One final note, if I may be so bold, knowing you are a man that likes to look ahead. If you are ever asked about forward planning for your funeral arrangements, could I suggest lead as a coffin lining. It's all the rage, apparently.

Yours sincerely,

Timothy Shift

Targeted Delivery Date: 25 September 1916

Clarence Saunders
% Piggly Wiggly
79 Jefferson Avenue
Memphis
Tennessee
United States of America

Dear Clarence,

Congratulations on finally opening your first Piggly Wiggly store earlier this month, after the initial delays with building work. I suspect you can already tell that it is going to be a real success, and change shopping for ever. Although a few others were toying with the idea, you are the first to really properly launch the self-service grocery store.

No need to wait for a crotchety old assistant, who should have gone to *eyeglass-savers*, to rummage around and fetch your goods. Rather, one can stroll through the turnstiles and then go up and down the aisles collecting what you want, placing your intended purchases in your basket. Is that why it is called Piggly Wiggly? Because you discover that, in fact, you spend most of your time going up, down and around the aisles searching in vain, and then realising that the one thing you wanted was actually back at the start?

You may be pleased to know that some modern superstores have taken your idea and truly perfected this approach. It has even reached furniture stores. For example, there is one known as IKEA where there are reports of shoppers being discovered a week after entering, dehydrated and desperate after being caught in the endless circulatory system, designed to ensure you have seen every single product in the store before you actually might have a chance to escape. Who knew that we were in need of so many small tables shaped like they came out of a jelly mould, with lamps to match, in shades of colour that even Turner would not recognise ("oh darling, that colour of *crimson-marigold-under-a-cloudy-sky-in-november* would go so well in the lounge"). Indeed, several people claim to have celebrated coming of age whilst being caught in the "IKEA-loop", although perhaps they are referring to trying out the bedding section after the store shut them in.

Still, your new system is causing a sensation in your first store - and although it does come with an increase in pilfering, the gains in efficiency and throughput seem to swamp that. You have even gone so far as to file for a number of patents around your new approach, including one for the self-service store concept itself, one for shelf-labelling of products, and even one for the idea of giving shoppers a printed receipt from the till. Today we take all these things for granted, and I find it amazing how much one person contributed to such a revolution.

I gather you have plans for rapid expansion and franchising - seems like the ideal way to go, once you have proved the model. Perhaps even more exciting are your thoughts around future store automation, which is essentially what we call the self-service checkout today - you truly are ahead of your time. I can assure you that such advanced automation trends will continue, to the point where, today, you can simply remove items from the shelf and place them in your own bag, and the store automatically knows what you have taken. I won't try and explain how that works, since the number of technical concepts I would have to introduce would cause us both to miss our tea and crumpets (aisle #4, bottom shelf).

Finally, one word of caution. If you are successful in the expansion you plan, you and your business will become famous. Any time a business seems like it is disrupting the status quo, it can become a target. There will always be those who might want to take you down or grab control, and are driven by the cash alone. You never know what is around the corner, and if the "takeover vultures" do start circling, often there is nothing you can do but fight the best way you can.

All the best for the future.

Yours sincerely,

Timothy Shift

Targeted Delivery Date: November 1988

Orville Redenbacher
Coronado
California
United States of America

Dear Orville,

With you being the face of popcorn on TV, adorned with your famous bow tie and glasses, many people forget that it was your agricultural science background that managed to actually create a new type of corn that would be more suitable for popping, back in the 1950s. Light and fluffy, as you say (every time). You now have your grandson in on the commercials - making it a nice two-hander - even though he had to change his name back to Redenbacher from Fish (since he was the son of one of your daughters) for advertising simplicity! Those TV execs can be pedantic, can't they!

I'll come clean on the point of my letter and say that I have a bone to pick with you. Yes, your popcorn is light and fluffy. Sure, it rises more than other brands and blows the lid of the popcorn maker (as you so often demonstrate). However, I am concerned over the level of reputational and financial risk you are running. It goes like this... people stream into the cinemas, buying buckets (the size normally reserved for bulk transfer of cattle grain) of your famous popcorn, and promptly spend the entire film crunching through it. In the darkness of the cinema, as the film reaches its climax, the crunching reaches a crescendo and that's when it happens. You bite into the one pesky un-popped kernel sitting in the bottom of the bucket and bingo, that's a cracked tooth right there. Now, the combination of a family set of cinemas tickets, your popcorn and a few super-sized fire-extinguisher grade drinks isn't exactly cheap, but that will be totally swamped by the cost of dental repairs. Given your focus on quality, I am surprised that these unpopped kernels slip through your control mechanisms. In fact, I might go further. Far be it from me to cast aspersions on the type of corporate sponsorship you have, but it seems to me that it would be in the financial interests of the American Dental Association for you to ensure there is at least one un-popped kernel per bag! Now, maybe I'm seeing saltiness where only sweetness exists, but one has to wonder. I'm not sure as to the level of public indemnity insurance that you are carrying, but it might be worth reviewing?

Ok, Ok, I know that you sold the company a long time ago and are now only the TV spokesman. In fact, you probably had no idea your product would end up in cinemas, and you have actually done some really amazing things in terms of philanthropy, but I just had to get that off my chest.

Finally, you may have heard of an emerging idea of being able to use computers to try and create digital characters for film and TV - even re-create those who have passed away. Eventually this will become very realistic, but early attempts will be fraught with problems and cause the characters to come across somewhat deadpan.* I'd have a chat to your grandson if you have any concerns and let him know what you think about the idea. It's never a good idea to overstay one's welcome.

Yours sincerely,

Timothy Shift

---

* Editors' note: We presume Mr Shift is referring to the Orville Redenbacher commercial (2007), available on YouTube.

Targeted Delivery Date: May 1942

Milton Snavely Hershey
The Hershey Company
Derry Township
Pennsylvania
United States of America

Dear Mr Hershey,

Without appearing sycophantic, may I add my congratulations to you for your philanthropic work, most especially regarding the orphanage school in Hershey.

I understand that at the start of World War II, the US Defence Department requested two chocolate bars from your company. The Ration D Bar and the Tropical Chocolate bar. I appreciate that the key feature of the latter is that it will resist melting up to 90 degrees. (Fahrenheit, I trust?!). Also, the other feature was that it should not taste *too* good. Those government boys want it to have an unpleasant-enough flavour to prevent the troops from developing cravings for them. It's an important part of their rations after all, but we don't want them scoffing the bars and feeling all lovey-dovey. We want them to finish their ration bars and to get up and want attack someone. Preferably the enemy.

Now, presumably you'll be employing taste testers for quality control during manufacturing production? There is a danger there of course - you know what it's like. You can get used to anything, and I would not be surprised if those tasters got kinda used to the sub-standard taste and may even develop a strong affinity for it.

My simple request is this, after the war, please, please can you make sure you employ a new team to taste the normal commercial bars for quality control. Round my way these days, there's been quite a few less than complimentary comments made about the taste of your Hershey Bars. I personally think that is just the regional differences in taste experience. All the same, I'd hate for your excellent brand to be devalued as a result of the sterling war effort work your company is doing, delivering twenty-four million bars a week. I wouldn't be surprised if you delivered a few billion by the time this war is over. Great work.

Anyway, I'm sure you'll take these comments in the spirit they were made, and thank you so much for you kind attention to my letter.

Yours sincerely,

Timothy Shift

Targeted Delivery Date: June 1897

Henry J. Heinz
Shrapsburg
Pennsylvania
United States of America

Dear Henry,

I am glad to read that your new company is thriving, after the unfortunate debacle of the first Heinz company (*Heinz Noble & Company*), which sadly went bankrupt. The good news is that the new venture, started with the help of your brother and cousin, seems to be going gangbusters. So much so that you have already bought them out, and the new company is now simply known as *H. J. Heinz*. You've been working on your marketing as well - good plan! I love the new tag line: *57 varieties* (ignoring the minor fact you are already making many more than that)! 57 has a nice authentic ring about it, right? Maybe it also resonates because I believe your lucky number is 5, and your wife's is 7? Nothing wrong in that - lucky numbers play a big part in both business and personal life in many cultures.

There is one new product you are launching that I wanted to ask you about, among all the various tomato ketchups and sauces - and that is baked beans in a tin. I assume this is broadly based on the traditional Native American recipes that have been handed down, with some simplifications for modern ingredients? I don't have any concerns with the recipe, but I am a little surprised to find that your first foray into the UK is to have your baked beans only stocked at the esteemed store of *Fortnum & Mason* of Piccadilly, London, with the product being sold as a high-end luxury item. Maybe I'm wrong about this, but expecting an order from the landed gentry for a case of Pol Roger 1892 along with a tray of baked beans just seems unlikely. I gather you are not stopping there in terms of product -

and you plan some additional varieties. One example stands out - to try and make it more attractive to the cherished bambinos of this upper-class market by adding fun little edible shapes into the product. Given your current marketing approach, what shapes are you thinking of adding? Little tiaras, silver spoons, Bentley cars & unicorns?

Look, I am sure you have done your market research, but I wonder if you might be missing a trick here? Families up and down the land are crying out for an easy, quick snack/dinner for the kids - and your baked beans (maybe spread over toast) could be just the thing. I like the edible shapes idea, but maybe adapt it and make it a bit more accessible - e.g. animal shapes, Disney cartoon characters etc.? (What's a Disney cartoon?...hmm, OK, make a note of that thought, so your company can react when they do appear). Plenty of co-marketing ideas there as well. Anyway, have a think about it.

Yours sincerely,

Timothy Shift

p.s. Ever thought about salads? They always seem somewhat dry... maybe something creamy to perk them up?

Targeted Delivery Date: October 1934

Elizabeth Magie (Philips)
Economic Game Company
58 West 68th Street
New York
United States of America

Dear Lizzie,

I believe congratulations are in order, on you receiving the 2nd patent for your inventive board game called *The Landlord's Game*, following your initial patent in 1908 (now expired).

Several things about your game are intriguing. First, I had thought that the idea of *gamification* was a relatively new phenomenon, but there you are at the start of the twentieth century teaching people economics and tax implications through a board game. I gather that a number of universities get their students to play it as part of their course! These days people are using gamification to try and encourage everything from saving the planet from drowning in plastic to beating your mates on the number of zits you can get rid of using only the rinds of rotten lemons. Sadly, the way things are going, the latter of those two looks more likely to be successful. The second thing is that you actually suggest two different sets of rules/ goals, and in each game the players decide which they are going to follow. One set of rules is where all players are rewarded by the total accumulated wealth, while the other set has the goal of personally gaining as much wealth as possible and forcing the others out of the game. I would love to know which set of rules were most popular? You have even started selling abroad, for example into the UK. For reasons that seem lost in the mystery of time, your UK distributor decided to change the game's name, and call it *Brer Fox an' Brer Rabbit*. And us Brits wonder why you Americans think we are so esoteric.

Of course, as you are only too aware, the path to more significant growth in popularity of your game is looking problematic. Despite you offering your game to Parker Bothers in the early days (and them turning it down), they are now launching their own game called, would you believe it, *Monopoly*, based on a supposed "new" game designed by Charles Darrow. Perhaps unsurprisingly, they chose the set of rules that call for players to try and force each other out of game, by building a "monopoly". You don't need me to tell you that this is pretty much a straight knock-off of your game, and they've done the dirty on you. As far as I can see, the only things Mr Darrow has contributed to the game are those funky drawings of the Jail and the Railway stations. Cute, but hardly enough to class it as a *new* game.

I realise you have had moderate success with a number of your other games, but it is a real shame that it looks like the big guys have won on this occasion. Although you may not be able to defeat them, always keep putting forward your side of the story. I think you should take some comfort in that, eventually, the world will come to realise that you were the driving force behind Monopoly.

Yours sincerely,

Timothy Shift

p.s. Please pass GO, and maybe collect $500 (if it is offered for, say, the patent)

Targeted Delivery Date: September 1873

William Blackstone
Indiana
United States of America

Dear William,

I gather you are working on a present for you wife's birthday next year. Now, I am all for planning ahead, but this seems a little over the top! However, I suppose inventing and building the first commercially available washing machine is a bit more involved than nipping down to the local produce store to buy the new edible sensation that has just become available - "solid eating chocolate".

I am sure you are aware of some of the recent advances in washing devices, namely James King (who filed a patent in 1851), although he is still trying to create a working machine. It sounds like he is close, and next year might be the year, so I would get a wiggle on if I were you. Then there is Hamilton Smith, who patented a different design in 1858 - so the competition is definitely out there. I gather your design is an enclosed drum with groves and paddles, in which you place the clothes, water and soap. Turn the drum by hand and hey presto, washing! Sounds ingenious to me. I guess the problem is someone still has to stand there and turn the drum.

I have heard rumour of some extensions to your invention that you are working on:

- A rope and horse harness that allows a spare shire horse to circle around the device, hence turning the drum.
- An improvement in the above technique, where two sets of shire horses circle in opposite directions, each moving alternately, giving the drum a nice back-and-forth motion.

I think the challenge for you is that while the above additions may indeed improve the cleaning of the clothes within your device, you will also need to work on inventing a carpet cleaner, floor cleaner and an industrial scale pooper-scooper, since all those shire horses in the kitchen are going to make a horrible mess. Frankly, I am uncertain if any of these will be successful, and you know what they say - sometimes "less is more", so you may want to consider launching an MVP (Minimal Viable Product) before looking at any enhancements. However, I am sure you know best, and I wish you good luck with your continued development. I believe you plan commercial production soon, with the intended retail price of $2.50. Seems like a bargain to me.

One final thought, and I hesitate to mention this, but you may not realise that you are starting an uncomfortable trend - where men give their partners a nice shiny kitchen appliance for their birthday. The expectation that this will result in them being overjoyed is quickly dashed, when they find that the partner actually sees this as simply reinforcing their place in life. Just a friendly warning...and perhaps have the details of a reliable florist to hand just in case?

Yours sincerely,

Timothy Shift

Targeted Delivery Date: 1978

Harland ('Colonel') Sanders
1337 Melton Drive
Lakeview
Mississauga
Canada

Dear Colonel,

My, but you've lived an exciting life. I am astonished by the several facets to your career, quite outside the fast-food business. Typically, I find myself writing to people who have known what their life's ambitions were from the outset, but you seem to buck that trend. I appreciate that "Colonel" is an honorary title conferred by the Governor but, after all, you deserved that honour at that time. I mean, delivering all those babies in Corbin, Kentucky. I understand that when questioned about this your only reply was, "There was nobody else to do it. The husbands couldn't afford a doctor when their wives were pregnant".

I was also most impressed by your aspirations to be the next Clarence Darrow. I believe you studied law by correspondence and practiced in justice-of-the-peace courts in Arkansas. It's a shame that a courtroom brawl with a client should have derailed your legal career. Most unfortunate.

Now, let me see if I have the next part of your career straight. You started serving food in a service station in 1930, but fried chicken was not on the menu because it took too long to prepare. However, you soon opened Sanders' Café across the street and began to serve chicken fried in an iron skillet. Food critic Duncan Hines included the restaurant in his 1935 road-food guide, and it was there in 1939 that you used pressure cookers to perfect your quick-frying chicken, coated in your secret recipe of 11 herbs and spices. A restaurant in

Salt Lake City, of all places, became your first franchisee. The Harman restaurant pioneered the famous bucket container and used the "Kentucky Fried Chicken" moniker. What most people associate with worldwide fast food today looked like a regional specialty on a menu in 1950s Utah.

So there you were, aged 65 and reliant on a Social Security check when you incorporated Kentucky Fried Chicken, and began driving your 1946 Ford around the country signing up new franchisees. Eventually you sold Kentucky Fried Chicken in 1964, and latterly food conglomerate Heublein purchased the company in 1971. We'll gloss over your lawsuit against Heublein for $122million where you accused them of selling 'slop'. I'm glad, at least, you settled that amicably.

An amazing journey without a doubt, but that leads me to the reason for writing and to ask for your opinion regarding one incident that happened back when you had your first diner. It's clear you never backed down from a fight, and I'm sure that served you well in the rough neighbourhood that surrounded your Shell Oil gas station. When you painted advertising signs on barns for miles around, your somewhat aggressive marketing tactic rankled Matt Stewart, who operated a nearby Standard Oil gas station. When told that Stewart was painting over one of your signs for a second time, you rushed to the scene with two Shell executives.

It is reputed that Stewart was the first to exchange his paintbrush for a gun. Also, that it was he who shot dead the Shell district manager Robert Gibson. I believe you returned fire and wounded Stewart in the shoulder. Stewart was sentenced to 18 years in prison for murder and charges against you were dropped after his arrest.

My question is this. Generalising, would you say that rushing round there with a gun was a good idea? I mean Mr Gibson from Shell is very dead. I'm speculating here but even if you were to offer his widow and children free KFC for life, while appreciative, I'm certain they would prefer he was alive and eating Big Macs even if they had to pay for them. Don't you believe that proliferation of firearms is a bad thing? In a way, the success of KFC has all turned on the result of a shootout.

I'm sorry I just can't get behind the "we were in the right - eat KFC" morality of the whole thing. Am I wrong? Am I missing something here?

Yours sincerely,

Timothy Shift

p.s. I'm also concerned about the hex you put on the Hanshin Tigers in Japan after the baseball fans celebrated a 1985 championship by tossing your statue, taken from a local KFC restaurant, into an Osaka river. I understand the team's subsequent championship drought has been blamed on the "Curse of the Colonel". Maybe it's time to lighten up a bit.

Targeted Delivery Date: December 1961

Ray Kroc
McDonald's Corporation
% MacDonald's Restaurant
Des Plains, Illinois
United States of America

Dear Ray,

Congratulations on completing the acquisition of McDonald's from Richard and Maurice McDonald. Although you have helped them run their franchise operation (based on their one San Bernardino, California store) since 1954, I gather that you have felt constrained by the owners' desire to keep the operation small - while you see a much greater future for the brand. Now you have acquired it (for $2.7m, ensuring $1m after tax for each of the founders), you are now free to drive the expansion. I know that it rankled you a bit that the owners kept the founding restaurant property as part of the deal, but hey, it's worth keeping your eyes on the larger prize.

What a strange small world it is - with both you and Walt Disney meeting all those years ago when you were both trainee ambulance attendants for World War I. Sorry to hear, however, that Walt turned you down for a McDonald's outlet in his new Disneyland resort. There is some confusion as to whether this was due to him demanding that you increased the price of fries from 10 cents to 15 cents, with him keeping the extra profit - something you were unhappy about.

I am wondering what your plans are for menu changes as you grow, while still focusing manically on standardisation to ensure a given product tastes the same whichever store one goes to? From your draft menus, I have gleaned some of the extra items you plan to add, for example:

- The McLobster - your desire to ensure that every American can eat up-market! Definitely worth a shot, I agree, although I just wonder if, when compared to a beef patty at 1/5th the cost, people will go for it? Also, won't the shell and claws be tricky in a bun?

- The McFly - the happy insect meal. While I commend you on being ahead of the game in terms of shifting away from traditional meats - I do wonder how your famed *Speedee Service System* would cope with that product. Given your desire for freshness, keeping tens of thousands of flies and bugs in a restaurant environment sounds like a recipe for disaster. Let alone having staff on minimum wage having to catch each one of the little blighters. However, if you do go for it, there are probably some movie endorsement options.

- The McHula Burger - a different attempt at non-meat, with a pineapple slice in a bun! It sounds kinda goofy! I also know that one of your franchise owners has some idea of fish in a bun (o-filet-of-fish or something like that). Here's my suggestion - put both on the menu and run a competition for a week or so, and see which one sells the most - keep whichever one wins!

Anyway, good luck with your new venture. I know that raising the funds was pretty tricky (given the level of debt in the business already), but my hunch is that your investment will pay off.

Yours sincerely,

Timothy Shift

p.s. Have you ever considered tennis sponsorship as a method of advertising? I think Big Mac might have an interesting angle there.

p.p.s. Keep up your interest in Baseball - always good to have a hobby for when you eventually retire.

Targeted Delivery Date: August 453 BC

Hanno the Navigator
℅ Magonid Family
Carthage
North Africa

Dear Hanno,

First of all, congratulations on completing your epic voyage by sea to explore the west coast of Africa, and map out potential new routes for the gold trade. A momentous achievement.

I hope this letter does actually reach you, since it has proved problematic to track you down. The first reason for that was entirely my fault. I spent quite a while communicating with a more recent countryman of yours of the same name who only seemed interested in elephants and their ability to survive altitude sickness. He didn't know his poop-deck from his rowlocks, if you pardon the expression. After I cottoned on that I had the wrong person, the second reason it has been hard to find you is that I am reaching back around 2,500 years. Not that my temporal messaging has any limits with time - but rather recorded history is annoyingly vague about exact dates the further back you go. So my targeted delivery date is a bit of a guess - if this reaches you, great, if it doesn't, well, you'll never know anyway!

Your voyage of exploration was remarkable. Taking sixty ships from Carthage, through the straights of Gibraltar, down round the uncharted west coast of Africa (and then getting home again), with basically nothing to really guide you, was outstanding. Today, even with the latest SatNavs, people still get lost and/or run aground all the time just moving around their local lake, so how you managed the coast of Africa is a mystery. In fact, one of the reasons it *is* such a mystery is that unfortunately your original account of your voyage has been lost. All that remains is a version of your ship's log (your *periplus*) that describes some details of the ports you visited. Unfortunately even this is a Greek version, copied from your original one written in Punic. And it's an *abridged* version, not even the full one! So we are almost, like, reading the tea-leaves here, you know (don't worry about that analogy if it doesn't make sense). I realise it's probably not a thing you worry about, but better recording of your voyage would have been a great help!

One of the controversies that a better record of your voyage would assist with is the question of exactly *how* far down the coast of Africa did you get? As far as Senegal? Sure, I think everyone agrees on that. Sierra Leone? Probably. Cameroon or even Gabon? Now things are getting pretty tenuous. Ironically, it mainly comes down to mountains. Is the one you describe in your periplus Mount Cameroon or Mount Kakulima, for instance? And what about the return voyage - the periplus we have doesn't even mention that!

One of the most fascinating things you report on are the fur-covered gorilla-people that you encounter on one of the islands. They fight like demons apparently? The women being just as ferocious as the men - three of which you captured, but unfortunately had to kill due to their violent nature. At least you brought back their hairy skins to be displayed in Carthage. I am sure you are hoping they will be safe there and be an example of your exploits. However, a word of warning - that upstart Roman Republic has always had eyes on Carthage, so you never know what's going to happen.

One final thing, I am sure on your long voyage you often looked up at the stars and moon. Fascinating and useful for navigation in equal measure. I'm not sure if you have given any thought as to how you might be remembered? Maybe, a crater on the moon named after you?

Yours sincerely,

Timothy Shift

p.s. You might be delighted to hear that, even in modern times, your exploits have been recorded in song (by a guy called Al Stewart). I think you would have liked it.

Targeted Delivery Date: June 1668

Dom Perignon
Benedictine Abbey of Hautvillers
Épernay
France

Dear Father,

I know that wine has always been an important part of many religious rituals and, as a monk, you must be familiar with a great many different kinds. Indeed, your knowledge in this area is well known, in particular things relating to the location and soil (known as the *terroir*), which can have such an impact on the grapes and the resulting wine. However, you really have taken on a Herculean task, if you pardon the expression, by agreeing to sort out the problems that they are having with their winemaking in the Champagne region of France.

You have seen the problem well enough - ask any cellar owner. Bottles exploding left, right, and centre, with glass shards injuring the helpless workers. So common is this issue that maybe only 10% of the cellar output survives each season! People have, sadly, been known to drink themselves to death, but being sent into the next world by an exploding bottle of wine before you had a chance to drink it, must be pretty annoying. I'm surprised the French military have not been in touch - since it sounds like they basically have self-made missiles right there....with admittedly somewhat random fuse timers. The cause of these exploding bottles - the bubbles that come from fermentation. So your mission, which you have chosen to accept, is to get rid of them! Pesky little things - just getting in the way of making some nice, albeit not that remarkable, still wine. The locals, known as *Champenois*, have always had a bit of a chip on their shoulder, eyeing the success of the Burgundy region, with the advantage they have of better weather.

I gather you already understand the problem, which is <u>double</u> fermentation. Basically, as the temperature drops over the winter, fermentation stops - so people think that's all done and dusted and it is safe to bottle. However, come springtime, and the weather warms up again, fermentation restarts and, well, kaboom! I'm sure you are already working on some cunning plan for removing these bubbles - but perhaps you should take a step back. Have a sneaky look at what the Brits are doing over there - they seem to be actually successfully making wine with bubbles in it...and enjoy drinking it! Crazy, right? Now, I know that in the eyes of a good Frenchman, those English have no taste, but maybe by accident they have discovered something? And why aren't they killing themselves off with exploding bottles, you might ask? Well, they may not have the vintner expertise of your countrymen, but they do have great glassmakers and know how to make good, strong glass bottles! In addition, they have come up with an ingenious way of sealing the bottle securely, using cork. Maybe give it a try, adopt some of these techniques, and see how the wine turns out with the bubbles left in!

Look, I know what you're thinking. If this works out, and wine from champagne with bubbles becomes a hit, you can't let it be seen that the English essentially enabled its creation. This would just cause so many problems, and before you could say "Moët & Chandon", a bunch of Kent winegrowers will be lobbying the leaders of Europe, asking to be allowed to call their wine *Champagne*. God forbid, next up they'll be saying they can make good cheese as well. So we will just have to try and keep this as our little secret.

Yours sincerely,

Timothy Shift

203

Politics & Humanities

Targeted Delivery Date: June 61 AD

Boudica
Watling Street
Britannia

Dear Boudica,

I have to admit this letter is a bit of a long shot, for multiple reasons. Ignoring the state of literacy in the first century AD for one moment, my first issue is that your whereabouts are somewhat vague. Usually, if you write to someone famous, even if you have just the street name, you can expect delivery. For instance, a certain Mr Claus gets his mail reliably and on time, and most letters only state the country! However, in your case, I understand that the postie might take issue - after all Watling Street is 276 miles long, being the Roman road from Rutupiae near the Kent coast all the way up, through Londinium (London), to Viroconium (which is in what we call Shropshire today).

The second reason for my concern is, and I don't know quite how to put this delicately, do you actually exist (well, as a unique person)? The descriptions we have of you and your exploits are all from the Roman side (and you know how the winners always like to re-write history). The story goes that your followers would shout your name as they ran into battle, but then *Boudica* is thought to derive from the Celtic word *bouda* - which just means 'victory'. This doesn't seem an unreasonable thing for the hoards to shout, whoever was their leader. *Tacitus*, the Roman historian, describes you as having a "huge frame, with a fierce aspect, a harsh voice, and long red hair". Basically, the ideal set of attributes most likely to distil loathing for the barbarians among the Roman readers, since they really hadn't got the equality memo yet. They still thought women should be demur, obedient, yet well read, but not to interfere in those complicated subjects such as politics and business.

Anyway, I'm going to hope for success and assume you receive this. You *really* have shaken things up! After the brutal treatment you received following your husband's death (and after the Romans decided, basically, to steal all of Norfolk, being unhappy with the half he left them in his will), your army has trounced the Romans left, right, and centre. Colchester - ransacked! London - burnt to the ground! St Alban's - flattened! I don't know if it will amuse you or alarm you to know that, today, there is a fine statue of you guarding the entrance to London. Yes, the very same town you totally destroyed. Nobody quite seems to see the irony these days, as they drive past it chatting on their mobile phones. By the way, don't worry what a mobile phone is for now, just think of it as a way of shouting across a large distance, while annoying those around you.

However, all good things must come to an end. And so it has, with defeat and the devastating loss of some 80,000 of your followers this year, somewhere around mile 226 on Watling Street, near Mancetta. Today, we call this road the A5, and there is a Little Chef restaurant nearby as reminder of tragedies past (plus a few they have produced themselves). You have managed to escape, but you must know your days are numbered. If I have this right, one source has reported that you might have chosen to be buried at a secret London location. Slightly unbelievably, this turns out to be the exact spot which, today, lies between platforms 9 and 10 of Kings Cross station. All I can say is that it's got to be getting super crowded in there. Are you any good at Quidditch?

Yours sincerely,

Timothy Shift

Targeted Delivery Date: 24 March 1895

Nettie J. Honeyball
% The British Ladies' Football Club
Crouch End
London, England

Dear Nettie,

First, commiserations on losing the inaugural match yesterday of the newly minted British Ladies' Football Club, going down 7-1 to "The North". You can't win 'em all, as they (will come to) say. Second, I hope you don't mind me calling you Nettie, since I'm aware that this probably isn't your real name? In that regard, we have something in common, since I'll come clean and admit that my name isn't really Timothy Shift, either.

For you, I gather, the name has proved a useful pseudonym to deflect the criticism and trolling you correctly anticipated receiving, from having the audacity to encourage women to play association football. So determined were you that you founded the club yourself, along with Lady Florence Dixie, and are its defacto first captain. I suspect that the crowd attendance at this first match (estimated at over 10,000) may have surpassed your expectations and delighted you. Perhaps not so good, was the heckling and general derision from most of the press. It appears that the art of writing insulting newspaper headlines is alive and well in 1895, with your young player Daisy Allen being described as "a small four feet goblin". "Unseemly" they also claimed, due to the fact that the team didn't wear corsets and played in standard men's boots (without high heels). Mind you, you did wear bonnets - and play was stopped should one become dislodged, so that it could be reattached. Bizarre how the press particularly think that women heading a ball will lead to the total moral breakdown of society. Hopefully you have already started to see that your approach to more appropriate attire is bleeding into the wider *Victorian Dress Reform* movement, and *suffrage* in general.

Of course, you probably already suspect some of the reasons for this negativity. Beyond just the sexism that you consistently endure, I think the men are just jealous you can attract such crowds on a shoe-string budget. The bad news for them is the cat is out of the bag, so to speak, and although the path to broader women's involvement in football definitely doesn't run smooth, there will be no stopping it. A century or so may need to pass, which may sound a bit depressing, but its coming of age in the early 21st century leads directly back to you, and the British Ladies' Football Club.

Actually, I'll take a punt on what I think your real name is. Many believe it might be Mary Hutson, Nellie Hudson or even Phoebe Smith, but I am going to go out on a wing and say I think you are Jessie Smith (née Allen). If so, don't worry, it will be our secret, and you can destroy this letter so that you remain anonymous for as long as you need to. You can probably imagine the conversation down The Maynard Arms in Crouch End if news of this letter leaked:

Man 1 - "Did you know Nettie Honeyball plays football and also got a letter from a time traveller from over a hundred years in the future"

Man 2 - "Good Lord that's astonishing. Plays football you say and she's a woman. I'm astounded"

Finally, I hope you enjoy your upcoming move to West Ham with your husband Fred Smith (brother of the Phoebe Smith mentioned above). West Ham, eh? I think you are going to like it.

Yours sincerely,

Timothy Shift

Targeted Delivery Date: December 1535

His Royal Highness, Henry VIII
Hampton Court
Near London
England

Your Highness,

Forgive me diving in, so to speak, but I wanted to make a suggestion regarding your 'Dissolution of the Monasteries'. As I understand it, your chappies have been running around closing down all the churches and bringing all the silver and gold back to you, with the dual aim of reducing the Church's power and influence as well as to bolster your finances.

The proposal I wanted to make relates to the fact that I believe you are missing a great opportunity regarding the real-estate. Currently, your men are smashing down the walls, breaking the windows and setting fire to the wooden pews. What you might not appreciate is the tremendous potential in terms of the value of these properties for assisted living retirement homes. In the 21st Century there is an immense demand for such properties, tastefully modernised of course, with comfortable rooms for people in their old age to live. They are publicised with pictures of luxurious swimming pools (that nobody, in reality, uses), happy chatting groups of old folk (hired from acting agencies, who themselves have seen better days), and in-house bistros serving home-made fare (which turns out to mean a choice between soggy fish and chips, and microwaved chilli con-carne). However, such residences are being snapped up faster than you can say *Archbishop of Canterbury*.

The advantage to you is this. In my time, most people approaching retirement age have to surrender their current home to pay for their place in a retirement home. With the average age of the population steadily increasing, the effective price they pay naturally diminishes. In your era, however, the average lifespan is significantly lower. You should therefore be able to get a much larger 'churn' on occupancy and so increase your financial rewards. If swimming pools and bistros aren't your thing, maybe include arm-char jousting and, food-wise, egret and swan roast dinners?

It's just an idea. Chew it over with your chancellor, Thomas Cromwell, and let me know via a letter what you think, and I'll prepare some plans for you to mull over.

By the way, maybe discuss the plan with Anne Boleyn. It will give her a head start on ideas for the decor etc.

Sincerely,

Your humble servant.

Timothy Shift

Targeted Delivery Date: September 1763

Jeremiah Dixon
% Plymouth Dockyards
Plymouth
England

Dear Jeremiah,

Congratulations on the new job - that's some gig you managed to get yourself! It isn't uncommon, throughout history, for people to have to travel a bit to find employment. Usually, it might be in the next town, or even a prosperous city in the same county - but no, this letter should reach you just as you prepare to set sail for the American colonies. Philadelphia, no less, to survey and confirm the dividing line between parts of Pennsylvania, Maryland, Delaware and Virginia. Not bad for a lad who was born and raised in County Durham, the son of coal miner.

I suspect it was attending John Kipling's School at Barnard Castle that drove your interest in surveying and astronomy, and enabled you to forge this new career. Ironic, really, that you should have been taught the skills that require such accurate vision at Barnard Castle, given its more modern reputation as a sanctuary for those with failing eyesight.

Of course, you will have your colleague Charles Mason with you on this endeavour - I am sure you two bonded well on your recent trip to monitor the transit of Venus across the sun. In fact, that probably gave you the travel bug, given that this wasn't done from your back garden between the potatoes and sweet peas, rather you had to try and nip down to Sumatra in Indonesia. Unfortunately, as often happens, you got attacked by a French warship en route, and because of the delay had to haul up on the Cape of Good Hope, South Africa and monitor the transit there. Travel delays are the worst, right? Full of anticipation at arriving at your destination, and then someone throws a spanner in the works. These days we moan like hell when there is 30-minute delay on the M25 near London, so next time that happens maybe I'll bite my tongue given what you went through.

I'd love to know how you are feeling, preparing for that voyage across the Atlantic. Trepidation, excitement, a little fear, maybe? Things aren't exactly running smooth over there, with talk of a revolutionary war. I am sure you know as well as I do that things like boundaries can become crucial in any disputes or hostilities that might arise. I suspect, however, that you are both just trying to concentrate on the job at hand. You already know that the first part of the dividing line is marked out with milestones - I have no idea why they felt they had to ship them all the way from England... don't they have stone quarries there? Anyway, you can start with these and then move out along the proposed new dividing lines.

I think you and Charles are also alert to the fact that, although you have some of the finest instruments the British Royal Society can muster, things often don't work as well in the field as they do in the lab. There's also the theory that the large mass in the nearby mountains might throw off some of your measurements - I guess you'll only know for sure if you don't end up back at the same place you started, when you trace your return route.

You probably don't even know how long you will be away - 4 or 5 years, maybe? I wonder if you have thought about how you might use the proceeds from your trip - I think the bill is going to be around £3,500. That's a tidy sum in the 18th century - always useful in later life. However, perhaps you are also hoping that this Herculean task is remembered in more ways than just financially. You know, maybe given a catchy name. I guess something like calling it the Mason-Dixon Line would do it, no?

Good luck for your upcoming voyage.

Yours sincerely,

Timothy Shift

p.s. One thing that might give you heart is to know that your exploits will be remembered in song - "Sailing to Philadelphia" by Mark Knopfler. I think you would like it.

Target Delivery Date: 105 AD

(Tshai) Cai Lun
Court of He Han, Honorary Title - Shang Fang Si
Manufacturing Instruments and Weapons
Guiyang, China

Most Esteemed Cai Lun,

I start this letter in ignorance of how to formally address you. I trust I correctly used your name, title and position in the Court of the Emperor He Han. Humble apologies if I made an error.

But never mind the words, what do you think of the paper? I went out and purchased the very best I could find. I really wanted to impress, you being the original inventor of paper. Just imagine receiving a letter and being able to say, "Oh, I invented this stuff". We all take paper for granted these days. It's one of the greatest inventions of mankind in terms of the difference it made, yet everyone just ignores it. It's invisible, an almost worthless commodity. I really don't know whether you are going to be shocked or impressed. Or both. Or neither. Anyway, I thought you'd like to be brought up to date on what's happening with your invention.

The basis for paper being so valuable is books. It has taken the best part of another thousand years until someone called Gutenberg came up with the idea of using a metal plate with words on them, splashed a little ink around and pressed on the page. Bingo - a book! Carl Sagan, an eminent astronomer once said:

> *"For 99 percent of the tenure of humans on earth, nobody could read or write. The great invention had not yet been made. Except for first-hand experience, almost everything we knew was passed on by word of mouth. As in the children's game*

"Whispers," over tens and hundreds of generations, information would slowly be distorted and lost.

Books changed all that. Books, purchasable at low cost, permit us to interrogate the past with high accuracy; to tap the wisdom of our species; to understand the point of view of others, and not just those in power; to contemplate — with the best teachers — the insights, painfully extracted from Nature, of the greatest minds that ever were, drawn from the entire planet and from all of our history. They allow people long dead to talk inside our heads. Books can accompany us everywhere. Books are patient where we are slow to understand, allow us to go over the hard parts as many times as we wish, and are never critical of our lapses." (Sagan, Druyan, 1995)

Quite an interesting insight from a man who spent his life staring up at stars. By the way, I read that quote in a book. He didn't tell me personally.

Without you, none of that would have been possible. I mean, parchment is great and all, but it was never going to scale. That's quite a legacy. Which got me thinking. It's 105AD right? Have you ever heard of a game called, Rock, Vellum, Scissors? Hmm, thought not.

Your sincerely,

Timothy Shift*

p.s. I'm frightened to even mention it, but the British wrap hot, greasy, take-away fish and chips in it. Sacrilege.

---

* Editors' note: Mr Shift also wrote to Johannes Gutenberg, and you can find his letter elsewhere in this collection.

Targeted Delivery Date: 30 March 1867

William H. Seward
Secretary of State
℅ The White House
1600 Pennsylvania Avenue
Washington, D.C.
United States of America

Dear William,

I believe congratulations are in order as today is the day you have finally completed the purchase of Alaska from the Russian Empire. Wow, most governments buy things like grain, ships or other products from abroad - you've bought a whole damn state (well, the makings of one anyhow). That's an additional 1.5 million square kilometres for the USA - equivalent to 3 new Californias! While I know there was general support for this idea, not everyone has been in favour. "Seward's Folly" they are calling it, or indeed referring to the whole region as "Seward's Icebox". Maybe your recent dice with death, when you (literally) dodged a bullet and survived the attack that assassinated President Lincoln, has given you the added impetus to just get things done?

Nice use of the British card, by the way. One of the reasons the Russians wanted to sell is they didn't think they could defend the territory from the Brits. See, we can come in handy, even now. I don't really want to question your motives, but you must admit this whole purchase thing is a rather handy diversion to get people focused on something else other than all the problems you are having with the Reconstruction, after the civil war. Turns out, I guess, that implementing the result of the war is almost as hard as fighting it. I mean, most politicians would arrange some kind of scandal as a distraction, something temporary so it can then blow over. Couldn't you have arranged the release of some story like, oh I don't know, maybe "President Andrew Johnson paid for a house on his duck pond using public money destined for orphans" or "Senior politician caught with goat in chambers" etc. I'm sure you could get creative. But, no, instead you went for spending $7.2m on a frozen land mass, where most of the current inhabitants are legging it back to Russia as fast as their huskies can pull them. Basically it's an empty wasteland, and it's a long time until Game of Thrones starts filming and needs such a landscape (and even then, the competitive bids from other countries will probably win anyway). Don't worry if you don't get that reference, it's just me trying to understand what drove you to this.

Despite my misgivings above, I will say that, in fact, your decision turns out to be pretty inspired. Could it be that you found some unknown internal memos that were filed as "unreliable" from the Hudson Bay Company about potential gold deposits in the Yukon area and beyond into Alaska? Most likely ignored, since everyone was sure the real money was in fur. Although you won't know this yet, I can let you in on a secret that there will be a serious gold rush around Nome in the years ahead....and it's all America's now! I don't even need to keep the specific location a secret, it's just all mixed in with the sand on the beach. The Russians will be kicking themselves. Mind you, not as much as they will in the future when they realise that us Brits weren't the ones to be worried about, and they threw away the advantage of having boots on the ground in the continent of North America. Just goes to show what happens when you play the short game.

All the best for the future.

Yours sincerely,

Timothy Shift

Target Delivery Date: 1st December 1815

Napoleon Bonaparte
Longwood House
Saint Helena
Atlantic Ocean

Dear Napoleon,

I must admit this letter took a very long time to reach you. It also took a very roundabout journey. It might seem strange my describing a letter taking a long time to reach you since it's been about 231 years in transit. However, it should have reached you a few years earlier than it has, but for a couple of silly mistakes I made.

First, (or last, depending on how you measure sequences in a time traveller's diaries) there was a stupid error on my part. I addressed the letter to St Helier on the island of Jersey instead of St Helena in the South Atlantic.

As if! Just imagine the British imprisoning you, the Emperor of France, on the British island of Jersey, less than 17 miles off the coast of France. I know it's a British island and all that, but we'd have had to send more troops to garrison the 'Bureau des Etrangers' to maintain our sovereignty. No, St Helena is the place. 1,500 miles west of Southern Africa and 2,500 miles east of Rio de Janeiro. Truly a slice of 'Old Blighty'. I imagine that you're really getting to experience the Britishness of the place by now, aren't you?

Oh, the original letter? Turns out that the postal workers' boss on Jersey is a bit of a Napoleon himself, so when the 'postie' saw the letter, he put two and two together and made five, thinking it was for the Jersey Post Office head honcho. I don't know where the original letter ended up, so when I noticed my error, I wrote again.

Not my first mistake. I addressed the next letter to Napoleon and it went to your nephew. Look. Some of this you'll already know. Some of this is going to be news which is why I thought I'd better go through things formally. I don't normally spill the beans like this, but after all, on this island in the Atlantic? Who you gonna call?

I hope you're sitting down. Your nephew Charles Louis Napoléon Bonaparte, (Yes, I know he's only about seven at the time you are reading this) will go on to be the first President of France from 1848 to 1852 and the Emperor of the French from 1852 to 1870. His regnal name is Napoleon III (I'm sure you're reading this with avuncular pride). He was, whoops, will be, the last monarch to rule over France. Elected to the presidency of the Second Republic in 1848, he'll seize power by force in 1851 and when unable to be constitutionally re-elected, he'll proclaim himself Emperor of the French. Cocky little devil, eh? Chip off the old block.

Anyway. He'll do loads of good stuff. He'll be popular. He'll oversee the modernisation of the French economy and fill Paris with new boulevards and parks by asking Baron Haussmann to redesign the city.

The thing is though, they really should keep him away from fighting wars. That's really not his thing. Yes, he's going to found the Second French Empire. Yes, he'll expand overseas and make the French merchant navy the second largest in the world. He'll even engage in the Second Italian War of Independence. But then, he'll only go and spoil it all fighting the disastrous Franco-Prussian War. He gets captured. Finito. Game over.

Actually, I have a confession. This is my fourth letter. My first got lost in St Helier. The second went to your nephew. The fourth is this letter you are reading but I have to say I made another mistake and a third letter ended up going to your son. Anyway, I know he has been Prince Imperial of France and King of Rome since birth but when you tried to abdicate on 4th April last year, you wanted your son to rule as emperor. It's a reasonable plan, but no. The coalition are not going to go for it, so I'm afraid Napoleon Junior, or Napoléon François Joseph Charles Bonaparte if you prefer, is only going to be Napoleon II for a short while. Just a few weeks actually. Besides he's in Austria now anyway. He'll be getting a new name soon. Franz, Duke of Reichstadt (I appreciate that title is not that of an Emperor but, you have to admit, it was really nice of the Austrian Emperor to have granted that, all things considered).

So now that I have finally reached you, I do have a question. More of a theory really. You are attributed with saying to your beloved first wife, "Not tonight Josephine". I believe that is a fiction initiated by the British to cast aspersions on your manhood. I wondered however, if it was perhaps half true? Had that quack medic, Dr. Alexandre Yvan, prepared another of his opiate potions for you that killed your ardour (*Wilt-agra*, perhaps)? You really should have said.

Anyway, hope I haven't been confusing you. Well, actually it's you Napoleons who are confusing me and practically everyone else I talk to. Talk about you Napoleons being complex!

Yours sincerely,

Timothy Shift

p.s. "Napoleon Complex". I'm sure I have heard of that somewhere before but can't place it. Any ideas?

Targeted Delivery Date: 1 June 1851

David Ochterlony Dyce Sombre
Kensington
London
England

Dear David,

It must be a relief to be back in England after the years abroad in
Europe. Not that your period of exile was really of your own
making, escaping the guards your wife had employed to imprison
you some eight years ago was probably the only choice you had.

It really is quite a tale, with you breaking the mould and being
elected as the first Asian Member of the British Parliment in 1841.
It must have felt great, getting 281 votes and defeating the
Conservative candidate with a swing of 25%. Both seats in Sudbury
going to the Whigs! Boy, would some politicians today like to be
able to pull off a swing like that.

Looking back, what a journey you have been on, literally and
metaphorically. From growing up in Sardhana, north of what today
is known as New Delhi, to visiting China, and then finally coming
to England and become elected as an MP. Your marriage, the year
before, to Mary Jervis (daughter of the 2nd Viscount St. Vincent)
was not without its own trials and tribulations, with you having
your concerns over her "socialising". But hey, all marriages have
their ups and downs, no? So there you were, a well married and duly
elected member of parliament, and then...it all goes to pot. First
the losing candidate objects to the election result, causing you to be
thrown out on accusations of bribery. Then your wife, aided by her
sisters, has you certified as insane and locked up, and cut off from
all aspects of your estate! I mean, talk about getting out of the
wrong side of the bed one morning!

Based on all that, giving your guards the slip and escaping to the continent seemed like a good plan; then spending the ensuing years traveling through France and beyond trying to prove your sanity and attempting to get the British courts to agree. That's the surprising thing, all the medics in Europe testified that you were perfectly sane. This is despite the fact that you had been eating copious quantities of Betel nuts which, in such quantities, can cause psychoactive effects, as well as taking various mercury-based "medicines" for ailments not entirely explained. I don't know if you have heard of the term "Mad as a Hatter", but this comes from the actions of hat makers after being exposed to mercury nitrate in the felt and other materials. There's a guy currently studying at Christ Church, Oxford, who likes to go by the name of Lewis Carroll, who is taking quite an interest in such things. You, however, against all the odds, seem to have come through this ordeal relatively unscathed (although that does kind of depend on whose side of the story you listen to). Although I am sure your whole time in Europe with these doctors has been frustrating, one thing you should feel proud of is that however (in)effective your drive to prove you sanity has been, it has caused a fundamental change for the good in how mental illness is investigated and described in Western culture.

So now you are back in England, and a new court case is set for a month from now, which you hope will finally clear your name. Please do try and look after your health as you await this hearing. The health and safety record of digs in London leaves a lot to be desired, with rusty plumbing and buckled floorboards with nails sticking out all over the place. As in all aspects of life, mind where you tread.

All the best in your upcoming court appearance.

Timothy Shift

Targeted Delivery Date: November, 1586

Sir Walter Raleigh
% The Court of Queen Elizabeth I
Hampton Court Palace
Greater London
England

Sir Walter,

I am quite confused, and I wondered if you could help me understand something.

First of all, though, it's fascinating to learn about what you Elizabethans call the 'New World'. That's called The Americas now. Anyway, lots of new places, new experiences and most of all, new produce to bring back to the UK. Heavens. This is England in 1584, and I just called it the United Kingdom. That's not for a couple of hundred years. Please forget I said that.

Anyway, I understand that Queen Elizabeth has granted you permission to explore, colonise and rule parts of the 'New World', in return for one-fifth of all the gold and silver that might be mined there. Gold and silver is your goal....and you bring back what? Potatoes and tobacco?

And sorry to let the cat out of the bag, but given this charter, **how come you've never even been there yourself?** I know you've been down to the Orinoco River basin in South America in search of the golden city of El Dorado. But America! Not to have been there even once. Such a shame.

If you change your mind and decide to go, check out further south down the coast of Virginia to a place called Florida. Bit swampy, but lovely and warm. In the far future, yours I mean, there's going to be a namesake of yours also called Walt, Walter Disney. He's going to be scouting out for a place called Disneyland which is going to be built just for fun. If we are talking about measuring the fun stakes - two weeks in Disneyland versus your contribution of french fries and a cigarette? I have to level with you, it's not even close - and Disneyland is unlikely to ever carry a government health warning. But who knows. Never say never!

Hey, don't worry, they'll name a city after you down in North Carolina with the catchy name of Raleigh N.C. In the meantime, don't start fretting over anything I've said. You won't lose your head over it. (...well not that issue anyway.)

Bye for now and give my best to your wife Elizabeth Throckmorton. Yes, I know you're married but don't worry - I won't tell the Queen. She'd be livid.

Yours sincerely,

Timothy Shift

Targeted Delivery Date: 497 BC

Confucius
Lu
China

zūnjìng de Confucius xiānshēng, (Most esteemed Confucius)

Please forgive these unsolicited comments; everyone knows you as the leading sage in China for your era. I also understand that you consider yourself a transmitter for the values which you claim have been abandoned in your time.

Your philosophical teachings emphasise personal and governmental morality, correctness of social relationships, justice, kindness, and sincerity, etc. That's all great, but your followers will have to compete with many other schools during the Hundred Schools of Thought era. You need to be aware that your teachings might be suppressed in favour of the Legalists during the upcoming Qin dynasty. It's very important therefore, to have sufficient wealth to support your teachings.

Specifically in this regard, I wanted to seek your personal views on your appetite for a sponsorship deal. I have never actually come across anything in print regarding your endorsement of any commercial products. That might just be my ignorance and not representative of your attitude.

Everybody knows your famous mantra "…. a journey of a thousand miles starts with but one step". For example, Expedia, who specialise in journeys of over a thousand miles, would be exceptionally keen to engage your services in promoting theirs. The value of having an 'A' lister such as yourself, would mean you could command a considerable payment for your recommendation.

I see the approach something like this:

> "Don't be Confused, Be Confucius.com" … or ….
> "A journey of a thousand miles begins with but one click on Expedia."

I don't want to get too bogged down on the specifics here. Let me know your reaction in principle and, if positive, I'll get my people to contact your people and move things forward.

Most respectfully yours,

Timothy Shift

p.s. Just in case Expedia doesn't appeal, how about acting as a Brand Ambassador for Rolex?

Targeted Delivery Date: 24 October 1901

Annie Edson Taylor
Bay City
Michigan
United States of America

Dear Annie,

Happy 63rd Birthday! Like most people, I gather you have something special planned to celebrate. Unlike most people, however, this does not include cake, balloons and too much jelly made in moulds of President William McKinley (God rest his soul). No, you're planning on making a real splash, literally! I'm not sure when you got the idea to get in a barrel and go over Niagara Falls, but it has certainly got everyone talking.

Look, I know you let your cat test it out a couple of days ago and, surprisingly, Bubbles came through relatively unscathed. However, recent human attempts are not exactly encouraging (Attempts: 3, Survived: 0), so if you make it, you will be the first!

It sounds like, despite the above, you are determined to go ahead - in which case all I can do is wish you the best. If by some miracle you do survive, make sure you keep tabs on that barrel - it will be famous, and it would be a shame if it was mislaid somehow.

Yours sincerely,

Timothy Shift

Targeted Delivery Date: August, 1649

James Ussher
Archbishop of Armagh & Primate of All Ireland
℅ Lincoln's Inn
Nr Chancery Lane
London
England

Dear Archbishop Ussher,

I felt I had to write to you at this time, as you are finishing off your blockbuster work *Annales veteris testamenti, a prima mundi origine deduct*, more commonly known as the "Annals of the Old Testament, deduced from the first origins of the world". Snappy title, and a weighty subject indeed. There's a lot of stuff in there, but the kicker is that you have given an update (following earlier attempts by others) for the exact date the world was created. I have to applaud you for the detail you have gone to in order to calculate this, by working backwards from "known" events. For example, how long ago was the temple built in Solomon's reign? How long between Abraham's migration to the date of that temple? How long between creation and that migration? Etc. There's real scientific rigour there - using the best available data you have.

The result is your new date - that the earth was created on the 23rd October 4004 BC. Naturally, you have also allowed for the standard pre-creation work required, so that the beginning of time was actually the day before - at 6pm on the 22nd. Now I don't want to rain on your parade, but I will hint that I believe you might be somewhat off. For one thing, while I appreciate we don't know exactly where the garden of Eden was, would the all-seeing Almighty really create the first two humans (naked, no clothes) at the end of October with winter approaching? However, I am really not here to criticise, given the data you have, and since I am not providing you with any new hard facts, it remains an excellent estimate. However, as time passes, and if your health allows, I would watch the progress of a young man called Robert Plot, who will become the curator of the Ashmolean Museum in Oxford. He may have access to some interesting large bones that were dug up near Chipping Norton - which are the first evidence that some huge animals might have been roaming around a long, long time ago, on a time scale that does not sit well with your new estimate. While it may take a while for everyone to appreciate what these new discoveries mean (and indeed the implications of the rocks in which these bones were found), pretty soon everyone will be in on the act. Even school kids will end up being able to find stuff on the beach that upends the established order of things.

As an aside, while I have your attention, and given your scholarly prowess at estimation, could you perhaps suggest 6 numbers (say, between 1 and 59) for a lottery competition I am entering? Maybe you could leave a hint somewhere in your papers?

Yours sincerely,

Timothy Shift*

---

* Editors' note: Mr Shift wrote to one such "school kid" (Mary Anning), and you can find that letter elsewhere in this collection.

Targeted Delivery Date: 24 September 1895

Annie Cohen Kopchovsky (Londonderry)
Boston
Massachusetts
United States of America

Dear Annie,

I hope you are relaxing and putting your feet up after your epic journey - the first person to cycle around the globe (and doing it in under 15 months). Please, no more, "I'm just nipping down the shops", for you for a while - keep the weight off those tired legs!

I don't know if you undertook this epic journey for the $5000 reward, just for the thrill of it, to prove what women can do, or simply because you had nothing better to do for a year or so. Whatever the case, it is impressive. Particularly so since, incredibly, I understand you had never actually ridden a bike until a few days before you set off! Talk about jumping in at the deep end. Did Albert Pope, who apparently put up the money (and by coincidence was also owner of the company that made the bicycle you started out on), brief you fully on what you were letting yourself in for? Or did he just take all the PR he was getting and actually utter the infamous words after the first day of "well, once you've ridden a bike, you'll never forget how to"? I suspect that around mile 15,756 that must have started to wear pretty thin.

OK, I realise that to win the prize you didn't actually have to cycle every mile across each continent, and so I know it has been said that it is perhaps more accurate to say that you travelled around the world *with* a bicycle rather than *on* a bicycle - but still, plenty could have gone wrong. Well, of course, plenty did. I am glad, for example, the French customs finally released your bike after impounding it. I also appreciate that a lot of the details of your trip through China and India might have been, err, gathered by your time on a boat nearby.

Whatever, you have certainly changed people's perception of women's cycling, the clothing they should wear and the essential items to carry with them. In your case it was a pearl-encrusted pistol. It is aways important to set our prepared for any eventuality, I am sure you would agree.

All the best for the future.

Yours sincerely,

Timothy Shift

Targeted Delivery Date: September 1780

Queen Charlotte of Mecklenburg-Strelitz
Buckingham House
London
England

Your Royal Highness,

I trust you have enjoyed your inaugural *Queen Charlotte's Ball* organised by your husband King George III, in honour of your birthday. As you stood there next to your giant birthday cake, and each one of this season's debutants were presented to you, I don't know if you realised that you were starting a trend that would last a couple of hundred years! At least it was all for a good cause, with the money raised going to a local London hospital (which, I am happy to say, will be renamed in your honour, to the *Queen Charlotte's and Chelsea Hospital*).

The tradition you have started is that the landed gentry and noble families will decamp from their stately homes and come to London for *the season* (which turns out to be half a year, ending in June when London becomes unbearable). As part of the season all the eligible new debutantes will be presented to the royal court, with the set of eligible bachelors being in attendance. Matches of convenience and mutual benefit will hopefully ensue. Today we call it *Love Island*, which has much the same goals but isn't really as classy.

One question I did want to ask was how did you indicate to each debutante whether you approved or disapproved of them? My understanding is that you would use some kind of a hand gesture? The old gladiator "thumbs up or down" is a bit passé - how about something like using your hand to *swipe right* or *swipe left*? You never know - that might catch on.

Yours sincerely,

Timothy Shift

p.s. How are you liking the new house? Sounds like you prefer it to St. James's Palace? If so, then why not work to make it a home suitable for a Queen and make it a bit more palatial - that would be a nice legacy, don't you think?

Targeted Delivery Date: November 1897

Florence Nightingale
Claydon House
Aylesbury Vale
Buckinghamshire
England

Dear Florence,

Everyone commends you for the great work you have done in elevating the sanitation and general hygiene in our frontline hospitals. Basic cleanliness is your mantra. I note that in your 1859 book, "Notes on Nursing", you raise the point "Every nurse ought to be careful to wash her hands very frequently during the day".

Forgive my presumption, but I believe I can clarify your message. In the event that you intend to publish an addendum to your book at any time, I wanted to suggest the following amplification. "Washing one's hands is so important it should be done for at least 20 seconds. An easy way to ensure this time is observed is to sing the song *Happy Birthday* twice".

This reportedly will be proved to be very effective during the Covid-19 outbreak in late 2019 and throughout the year 2020.

On reflection, I realise that you'll possibly not be familiar with the song lyrics, "Happy Birthday". However, I'm certain you'll have heard the song "Good Morning to All", since it was published in 1893. In 1931, the lyrics will be changed to "Happy Birthday to you" and become the most popular song ever written. I'm probably confusing the issue here, so you can just go ahead and sing:

> Good Morning to you.
> Good Morning to you.

Good Morning dear children.
Good Morning to all.

or

Happy Birthday to you
Happy Birthday to you
Happy Birthday, whatever you name is.
Happy Birthday to you.

I understand either set of lyrics are equally efficacious.

I do hope you find my suggestion useful and a worthwhile point to make.

Most sincerely,

Timothy Shift

p.s. Don't get too excited about this insight into a future song. Nobody pays a blind bit of attention to the copyright. Patty and Mildred Hill might just as well not have bothered.

Targeted Delivery Date: January 601 AD

His Royal Highness, King Arthur
℅ Tintagel Castle
Camelot
North Cornwall, England

My Liege,

I hope that this communication reaches you. I had immense difficulty finding an authoritative address since, strangely, the postman didn't actually know the location for Camelot.

Anyway, I wanted to add my voice to the throng who praise you on the creation of the egalitarian society over which you now preside. Your round table meetings with your noble knights are the stuff of legend. With such a strong precept of fairness and chivalry it would be a brave, or perhaps a stupid, man who would question your approach.

So at the risk of upsetting you, have you considered feminism? With all those testosterone-fuelled grand knights around the table, would it not be appropriate to have the round table with both men and women? Just to have a more balanced approach.

Not to cast any wild aspersions but, just saying, if Lady Guinevere were brought into the decision-making process, she might spend less time just combing her tresses and entertaining your knights. Now, I don't suggest for one minute that she's playing the field, but it would be good to steal a march on any future government directive to have balanced gender equality in the boardroom. Hope you don't mind a little constructive criticism. History just doesn't record your views on such matters.

Perhaps I might crave a little more of your time. I know you are really keen on this idea of round tables - it makes everyone equal, no head of the table etc. I just wonder if perhaps you a missing a trick in terms of the wider benefit to your subjects?

Now, you are probably already ahead of me on this, since while your average castle isn't short of space, fitting a round table into your typical subject's one-up, one-down home would be challenging. This is where your role as a leader in post-Roman Britain comes in - maybe you should shake up the table manufacturing industry with new methods? How about starting a trend in, say, flat-pack furniture? Imagine your loyal subjects being able to afford their very own, fold away round dining table - it would be a great boost to limited space, as well as fostering family communication. I am sure you will agree, it would be far better for families to all eat together, rather than everyone eating their food on their lap staring at a square box drawn on the wall. You could be seen as a real trend setter!

I believe there are some novel craftsmen out in Sweden and Norway that maybe could help with the design. You could give it a catchy name, you know maybe like International King Arthur Enterprises (IKAE), or something close to that. It could really go down a storm in both England and Europe. "The Arthur Table. Designed in Sweden, Made in Camelot" has a nice ring to it, no? In addition, building trade with those Northern European counties might prevent any further unwanted hostilities. Given that France seems to be claiming you for their own, they'll probably like the idea as well.

Anyway, I'll leave you to mull over the idea to see if you could be known as the ruler that improved everyone's habitat.

Your humble servant,

Timothy Shift

Targeted Delivery Date: 13 March 44 BC

Julius Caesar
Curia Julia
Regio VIII Forum Romanum
Rome
Roman Republic

Hail Julius,

I am having such a difficult problem getting in touch with you. At first, it was just getting the post office to accept a parchment scroll with a wax seal. In the end they agreed to take the parchment, but the wax seal was a complete no-no.

The bigger problem is that I don't know what day it is. Many people have been saying that about me for years, but I mean it literally. I thought it was March 13th (Gregorian calendar), but I understand that you think it is March 15th (Julian Calendar).

Best thing you ever did was to reform the calendar replacing the lunar calendar with the Egyptian calendar, which is based on the sun. Roman farmers are now able to use it for consistent seasonal planting year to year. Setting the length of the year to 365 days was spot on and adding a leap day at the end of February every fourth year is a nice touch. Now your calendar is almost identical to mine.

The problem is, I use the Gregorian calendar introduced in October 1582 by Pope Gregory XIII as a modification to your Julius Caesar (Julian) calendar. The principal change will be to space leap years differently so as to more closely approximate the 365.2422-day 'solar' year that is determined by the Earth's revolution around the Sun.

OK, so hold on to your laurel wreath, it's not really that difficult:

- Every year that is exactly divisible by four is a leap year
- Except for years that are exactly divisible by 100
- Except those centurial years that are leap years if exactly divisible by 400

For example, the years 1700, 1800, and 1900 are not leap years, but the years 1600 and 2000 are, were, or will be depending on whether you're you, me, or Pope Gregory. Clear as mud, eh?

I know what you're thinking. What does it matter if I'm sending letters back in time? Well, it matters big time. Get it wrong and you're messing around with the time dimensional flux. Or 'timestamp' as some people like to call it. You'd get the letter, but the page would be blank. No writing on it at all. (Marty in 'Back to the Future' knows what I mean).

Anyway, if you can read this I've got it right, but if history never recorded you having received this parchment I blew it. Or maybe you were just busy today.

Yours sincerely,

Timothy Shift

p.s. Beware the Ides of March

Targeted Delivery Date: October 1803

Prince Frederick
(The Grand Old) Duke of York and Albany
Oatlands
Weybridge
Surrey
England

Dear Frederick,

First, I am not at all sure if I have found the correct Grand Old Duke of York. History is a bit vague as to which one the nursery rhyme is referring to. While you seem to be the most popular, there is also Richard, the Duke of York (1411–1460) as well as James II (1633–1701), formerly the Duke of York. There is also a much more recent Duke of York who would have dearly loved to be able to inspire 10,000 men to follow him, but not much chance of that now. There is also a French version of the rhyme where somewhere between 40,000 and 100,000 men are involved, but European budgets always have a habit of getting escalated, leading to a lot of irrational decision-making.

So, assuming I do have the correct Duke of York, I wanted to see how you were feeling after the somewhat disastrous Flanders campaign. One question I do have is that given the Dutch landscape was so flat, what was the rationale for marching all those men up the only hill for miles (at Cassel), and then down again? I mean, it was only 150m or so high! It didn't achieve anything, and then you had to withdraw anyway! I fear you have started a trend of military forces being moved around, to no end, bringing no advantage, whether on open plains or in trenches - and people will stick your name on it.

The only piece of advice I can offer you is to try and step back and analyse what were the real reasons for the failure of the campaign. What changes does the British Army need to make in order to be fit for purpose in the coming Nineteenth century? I'm glad to see a totally ineffective and failed campaign never held anyone back, and so in your newly appointed role as Commander-in-Chief maybe you might be able to make some of the changes needed? For instance, do you think that officers are sufficiently well trained? Perhaps they need their own college? There's some land going begging over at Sandhurst - maybe not a bad location?

Finally, and not wishing to intrude in one's private life, but I do have some concerns regarding your latest muse, Mary Anne Clarke. Comely as she may be, I'd be a little cautious with some of her business dealings. Rumours of Cash-for-Honours has bedevilled more than one Duke of York.

Yours sincerely,

Timothy Shift

Targeted Delivery Date: 16 May 1903

Albert Mansbridge
Battersea
South London
England

Dear Albert,

I just had to write to you on this day, since today is the start of something that will affect an incredible number of lives. Is this some new medicine? No. Some new scientific invention? Nope. Instead, you and your wife (Frances) have just stumped up the princely sum of two shillings and sixpence, from the housekeeping money, to start a new initiative that will change education across the country (and, in fact, many countries of the world). You have called it *The Association to Promote the Higher Education of Working Men*, which (and I'll let you in on a secret) will eventually become known as the, more manageable, Workers' Educational Association (WEA). Driven by your unhappiness that existing extension/evening classes were primarily focused on the upper (or at least middle) classes - you saw the need for something that is more appropriate to the much greater number of working men. What you are starting here will, I can assure you, revolutionise learning for people (both men and women) already in employment, and those that desire to be. It will lead to literally millions of adults bettering themselves by taking evening classes - something that continues to this very day. Not a bad return on the housekeeping money, eh?

The courses you start, while initially limited, will mushroom into a wide variety across many domains. I know you are still working on your first prospectus, and you are naturally focused on the advancement for those in the industries of your time. However, I do wonder if a few of those you propose in the draft prospectus are a step too far? A few that stand out in this category are:

- From Quickstep to Charleston for Steel workers (Instructor: Teddy Balls)
- Soufflés for the common man (Instructor: Barry Merry)
- Improved Coal Abstraction (Instructor: Arthur Cutgill)
- Modern factory and workforce relations (Instructor: Scarlet Robbo)
- Ornamental garden lawn irrigation design for Textile workers (Instructor: Alan Smallbog)

Perhaps you might consider amending these before the final version is published?

The above aside, as the English philosopher Herbert Spence said, "The great aim of education is not knowledge but action" - something which I suspect you would wholeheartedly support and intend to be the result of your work. I wish you good luck in your endeavours.

Yours sincerely,

Timothy Shift

Targeted Delivery Date: 325 BC

Aristotle
The Peripatetic School
The Lyceum
Athens
Macedonian Empire

Dear Aristotle,

Greetings! I am writing to you at the Peripatetic School, firstly to congratulate you on all you have achieved in your teachings and studies across such a wide variety of disciplines. Here in the 21st century AD (that's about 2,350 years in the future for you), you may be delighted to hear that you are still considered as the "Father" of many such disciplines, including logic, political science, physics, ethics, scientific method and realism to name just a few. Even though most of your writings were not intended for publication (rather to simply aid teaching), many fragments have survived, either directly from you or your students. Sadly, some of your writings are lost forever - and of course, it is hard for us to tell which ones! However, you are considered one of the world's first polymaths!

Of course, in the same way that you have modified the views of your teacher Plato, I am sure you will not be surprised to learn that your own ideas have been adapted over the centuries. I have no doubt your views on the fact that everything is made up of only five elements (Earth, Water, Air, Fire & Aether) made sense at the time, but unfortunately things didn't work out quite that simple. Setting such minor issues aside, and despite our great distances in time, I am writing to you to ask for help! Your teachings are so broad that they relate to many aspects of politics, debate and government. Despite the evolution of how governments and democracies are run since your time, there is a general feeling that we are now going backwards again. You may be discouraged to hear that many of today's political systems are gripped by popularism, built on the basis of half-truths and lies which, when repeated often enough, gain the validity required to endorse those telling them. Truth and Realism are in short supply.

For centuries, those in power often got away with running the show with false narratives without much opposition - primarily because there was no effective and timely way of disproving these narratives. Then in the last fifty years or so, with advent of planetary-wide instant communications, many such regimes started to fall from grace since their lies were exposed. To misquote a famous saying, you could no longer fool many of the people, much of the time. Before we go on, you probably want to know what is a *planetary-wide instant communication* system? Well, without getting technical, just imagine that you could write one of your dialogues (say, on Politics), and then <u>in an instant</u>, everyone across the Greek empire (or even across the world) could read it. Not only that, but they could ask you direct questions without having to come to your school - you could *hear their questions* (and answer them), from their homes or places of work. In fact, you could also *see them* and they could *see you*. Further, anyone in the Greek empire or beyond, could publish their own dialogues to put across their point of view. Seems like the work of the Gods I hear you say, but in the late 20th century AD humankind created such a system.

Your mind is probably already racing at the implications of such a system - and you might think that it would have created a basis for common understanding of what is true and real. Sadly, in fact, that promise has not been fulfilled. Such is the volume of information now being published, many people struggle to understand what is real and what is fake - which nefarious politicians across many countries have now blended into their political narrative. They have discovered that they can still say whatever untruths suit them, and if they say (and publish) them often enough, people can be persuaded to accept them - even if there are counter arguments which are backed by far more credible witnesses (available to everyone).

Fundamentally, despite all our advances, people are still far more persuaded by what they *want* to believe, fuelled by herd mentality, than what the weight of evidence suggests.

I'd love to know if you have any advice and guidance that you might be able to provide us? Despite all the changes to society and technology, you would find people in the 21st century AD very similar to those in the 4th century BC. Could you perhaps elaborate as part of your dialogues on *Ethics* ("the potential to be happy requires a good character"), or in *Politics* on your proposal for a model of voting that combines one-person, one-vote with some kind of merit-weighted attributes? Or perhaps more generally on methods for a shared understanding of realism and truth?

In essence, how can we find ways to ensure the evidence of experts is not simply refuted by beliefs that just don't stand up to such evidence? Could perhaps your idea of *weight-of-merit based opinion* be used to enable this? Or course, you might well argue, that this just transfers the problem to the choice of who you select as experts! However, in a world where almost nothing goes unseen and there are many hundreds of thousands of independent experts in any field, could not a *herd of independently accredited experts,* from a cross-section of schools such as yours, be entrusted to provide such merit-based opinion? I live in hope for any views you may have on the above in your writings.

Yours, hopefully,

Timothy Shift

Targeted Delivery Date: February 1555

Michel de Nostredame
Saint-Remy-de-Provence
France

Dear Nostradamus,

It may come as no surprise to you that I suggest that we stop the correspondence for the time being. Your reputation as a foreteller of the future, clairvoyant, futurist, call it what you will, is wholly based on the pretext that you are solely responsible for your perceptive commentary.

Frankly, I am having trouble and to be honest just plain fed up, keeping up with your persistent requests for information of what happened next. Your letters seem to be never ending and designed only to keep Catherine de Medici happy and better serve her meddling in French politics. Enough is enough. I have a life too.

I suggest for now you tell everyone to stop asking you for portents of the future because you are quietly contemplating what might happen next. In fact, I recommend that you leave it that way until, say, 3rd July 1566.

~~Best regards~~ Sincerely,

Timothy Shift

p.s. I bet you didn't see that coming!

Targeted Delivery Date: September 1954

Sir Winston Churchill
Chartwell House
Westerham
Kent
United Kingdom

Dear Sir,

I hope this letter reaches you during your 2nd term as prime minister. Although I have so many questions for you, for now I must leave these to a subsequent letter.

I write on this occasion on a relatively sensitive subject. I have recently been contacted by representatives of a top-tier Cuban cigar supplier, who apparently did business with you. Whilst they describe you as one of their finest customers, they tentatively brought up the subject of one unpaid bill that appeared to have been overlooked. This was for partial re-stocking of your 3000-4000 cigar store at Chartwell. They suggested that the usual arrangement of you leaving the payment under the empty milk bottles in the morning had always worked impeccably, so they are at a loss to suggest why this one bill was missed. Was it nefariously taken by someone else, perhaps in a bid to discredit you? They mentioned reports from the time about a chap who was seen loitering around who looked a bit suspicious. Name of Aden or Eden, I believe? Perhaps that means something to you?

Since your love of Cuban cigars is well known (particularly *Romeo y Juliete* and *La Aroma de Cuba*), after you first tasted them in 1895 while visiting there, the company in question would not want anything to spoil this relationship. Since by 2046, this relatively small bill has, with compound interest, exceeded several millions of pounds, perhaps you could again pop out payment tomorrow with the milk, so this can be self-erased from their records?

Yours sincerely,

Timothy Shift

Targeted Delivery Date: 6 August 1926

Gertrude Ederle
Kingsdown
Deal
Kent
England

Dear Gertrude,

Please accept my apologies for the poor welcome you received on your arrival in Kent. I am sure you can appreciate that it is customary for anyone from abroad to be asked to produce their passport upon first setting foot on British soil. However, I have to say that the customs officer in question somewhat overstepped the mark, given that your arrival on the beach in Kingsdown was due to the fact that you had just become the first woman to swim the English Channel. I guess to be fair to him, few tourists arrive covered in goose fat.

On a positive note, however, not only have you become the first woman to complete this feat, but you beat the fastest time of any of the five men who had swam it previously by 2 hours! The *Queen of the Waves*, they are calling you! That's a shot in the arm for women's swimming. Sounds like you did the right thing by designing your own swimsuit, rather than using the totally inappropriate woollen female bathing costumes of the time. At least you didn't get arrested for wearing a suit that failed to cover your legs, as was the Australian swimmer Annette Kellerman some years ago in Boston.

I don't know you if you realise it yet, but you'll be famous by the time you get back to your native America. Ticker-tape parades, etc. Enjoy it, soak it in - because sadly this kind of fame often doesn't last. There's always some other record or technological feat of daring around the corner that can make today's famous names into yesterday's heroes. You never know, next we will find that someone flies the Atlantic or something.

Congratulations again on an amazing swim.

Yours sincerely,

Timothy Shift

Targeted Delivery Date: Monday 23 May 2022

Doowy, Suem and Howe
Attorneys at Law
Temple Bar Chambers
Temple Bar
London EC1
United Kingdom

Ref: Your Client - Mr Maximus

Dear Mr Doowy,

I am in receipt of your letter dated Friday 20 May 2022, but I am afraid we cannot comply with your cease and desist order for the reasons outlined below.

I understand you represent Mr Maximus, who is a medium and I believe has an exclusive agreement with certain clients with whom he intends to communicate once they have died. Accordingly, you consider our client Mr Shift's letters of communication with these people to be interposing with the exclusive contract(s) Mr Maximus already holds with them.

I quite understand Mr Maximus' concerns, but be assured, any communications from Mr Shift to Mr Maximus' clients, were only made, and will only be made, whilst his clients are, or more correctly I should say, were, still alive.

I will concede that in one instance, a letter to Methuselah arrived sometime after his death but that was only because of wildly inaccurate information regarding his age when he died. Mr Methuselah's death had been reported quite incorrectly in otherwise well respected, authoritative written documentation. Unfortunately, he was well dead when he (would have) received our client's letter.

Naturally, once we learned of this error, Mr Shift wrote again to Mr Methuselah but this time before he died. It is most unlikely that this error will happen again. I don't even believe Mr Methuselah was a client of Mr Maximus.

Yours sincerely,

Mr C. Ewan Court
Legal Representations LLP
For and on behalf of Mr Timothy Shift.

Epilogue

So, there we are. That's almost all of the first batch of letters that Mr Timothy Shift sent to us. We hope having read these letters, your reaction is more positive than on starting this book. As for our friends whom we falsely accused of playing a prank on us, even they are starting to see us in a different light.

Frankly, we sincerely hope that Timothy Shift, or whoever he really is, sends us some more material to publish. We so enjoyed the task and are grateful for him choosing us as his cohorts.

And if you too enjoyed reading these letters, we saved one letter for last.

"Just one more thing........."

Targeted Delivery Date: August 2001

Steven Jobs
CEO and Founder
Apple Computer Inc
1 Infinite Loop
Cupertino CA
United States of America

Dear Steve,

"Insanely great". That's a hell of a phrase. Many people get hung up on such comments and choose to criticise when they have no basis to do so. Benjamin Disraeli, the British Prime Minister to Queen Victoria famously said, "Success is an unremitting attention to purpose". I think that fits well with your own mantra, doesn't it?

And me? Am I in a position to be judgemental? Well in my case, my 'received wisdom' comes from the fact that I'm from the future. It's easy being smart when you know what the outcome is. Sure, we all know that you can be a bit abrasive when you are focusing on an issue. More than a tad obsessive too. But how would you be expected to behave? Does turning up each day, working hard and being nice to everybody eventually create a company with the highest share valuation in the world? Well, we both know the answer to that question, and if on the journey you rub a few people up the wrong way, that's how it goes.

Anyway, I digress and I'm not writing to you to blow smoke up…. well you know where. I'm a long time Apple user. In truth, the longest Apple user you'll ever hear from, but you'll have to take my word on that. I just thought that due to my extended patronage and that I too have a rather futuristic, Reality Distortion Field, that earns me the right to chip in a couple of comments. And let's face it, you're a man who can recognise the future when he sees it.

People have criticised you for, how should I say, leveraging other peoples' visions of the future. For example, the Apple computer mouse is wholly based on the interface and mouse that you saw up at Xerox's PARC Labs in Palo Alto. Wasn't that just what you were looking for - even if you didn't know it until you saw it? My view is that it is unfair criticism that you stole it. PARC Labs may be a world-renowned think tank, but thinking alone doesn't sell hardware. How many Xerox computers do we see today? None. It was the best thing that you brought it out into the open and put better focus behind it.

Then there were your endeavours at NeXT Computers when you had your little, err, sabbatical from Apple. Then the Apple board asked you back with "Sorry Steve, we didn't mean to fire you. We love you really. Please come back and help us run the company and by the way, could you bring your NeXTStep operating system with you?". It was an irresistible offer really driven in no small part for their dire need for a real operating system. I personally think it uncharitable that several people made the unkind comment that all you had done was to lift it from others. I know it was wholly based on Mach that had been developed at Carnegie Mellon University by Richard Rashid and Avie Tevanian, but you hardly stole it. Avie joined you at NeXT and again at Apple as CTO.

Well as you are a tech visionary who loves and understands the commercial value of tech, I just love your reaction to the Apple Newton MessagePad. A Personal Digital Assistant with a screen and a stylus that allows you to write on the screen whatever you want. Calendar, Notes and Addresses and even connect to the Network. What's not to love? Well, apparently everything. You axed that gismo within days of arriving back at Apple. "I've seen the future and it's not the Newton" you told the press. Well, I have to admire your focus and resolve. Man, you have some chutzpah. Here you are, Chief Futurist Officer at Apple (well actually, every job at Apple with a "C" in front of the title) and you throw the MessagePad away, along with the millions in development and production costs. Hey, I'm from the future - I don't have a crystal ball. I just have 20:20 hindsight because I know what happens next. You, my friend, just follow your instincts and your instincts are that this the Newton is 'toast'. Well, you're going to be proved right. Whoops. That privileged information just slipped out, but what the hell. That's probably one of the things people don't know about you - most folks see you as famous for inventing and building new things (and that's partly true of course), but I've always felt your key strength was deciding what NOT to build. So many companies keep poor products hanging around simply because they can't make the hard calls to shut them down - but not you!

So, what next? I suppose I might as well be hung for a sheep as a lamb. A guy called Tony Fadell might knock on your door. He has plans for a music playing gizmo - a device that will make Sony Walkman cassettes and Sharp MiniDisc players look positively prehistoric. Bring him onboard. Tony's hardware visions don't grow on trees and visions certainly don't come to you in dark rooms just by thinking hard. You've proved that yourself by grabbing opportunities with both hands. So get grabbing. It will need a snazzy name, of course. You already have the iMac - and if someone spots the analogy between the small exploration Pods on the Discovery in *2001: A Space Odyssey* and this new device, maybe use that to craft the name? This will become a template for the Apple future and more "Cosmic Stuff" that you'll bring to market.

So, while I'm in the mood to 'spill the beans' let me make a couple more suggestions. First, at every annual product presentation, you need a look. A standard statement that is instantly recognised. What about, from now on, you always wear the same style of black T-Shirts? The famous designer, Issey Miyake does a fantastic line in these, and well, they're not cheap so you'll be able to keep ahead of the pack. Your computers and other stuff can come in every colour of the rainbow, but perhaps not you. Hey, that's one less thing to think about getting dressed every morning. Keep that focus for the job!

Second, now that you'll have perfected the look, why not pep up your product launches. How about a trademark tag-line for your presentations. Keep something up your sleeve. Keep the audience begging for more and more, 'stuff'. Tease out their lust for technology. Have them pleading for products and gasping for gizmos and save the best for last. Just precede it with;

"...and just one more thing...."

Bam, your stock just went up 10 points!

All right, perhaps those last two pointers are not mega but finally, do me, yourself, and all those dear to you a favour. Listen to your own body. If you don't feel well, see a doctor. Quickly and preferably one in a white coat just up the road from the world renowned Stanford Medical School, rather than rely solely on alternative practices. I appreciate your desire to 'Think Different', but sometimes, just sometimes, being conventional works better.

Trust me, I too have seen the future.

Yours sincerely,

Timothy Shift

Acknowledgements

Undertaking any book is one of those tasks that starts out as a simple idea, and morphs into a complex and much longer term project that you ever imagined. We have had fantastic people supporting us and offering advice, during this process, including Leigh Share, Maureen Morris, Richard Bailey, Joni Lloyd-Bailey, Thomas Bailey, Emma D'Arcy, Helen Thacker, David Port, Nicola & James Hogan, Julia Jameson, Anne Murray, to name just a few (and we are sure we have forgotten many). Finally, of course, our partners Denise and Susan.

Despite the best efforts of those listed above, any errors that remain are ours alone.

Citations

Adams , Douglas , *The Restaurant at the end of the Universe*, 1995 , Del Rey , Paperback

...One of the major problems encountered in time travel is not that of becoming your own father or mother. There is no problem in becoming your own father or mother that a broad-minded and well-adjusted family can't cope with. There is no problem with changing the course of history—the course of history does not change because it all fits together like a jigsaw. All the important changes have happened before the things they were supposed to change and it all sorts itself out in the end...

...The major problem is simply one of grammar, and the main work to consult in this matter is Dr. Dan Streetmentioner's Time Traveler's Handbook of 1001 Tense Formations...

Sagan , Carl and Druyan , Ann , *The Demon-Haunted World: Science as a Candle in the Dark* , 1995 , Random House , Hardcover and Paperback

...For 99 percent of the tenure of humans on earth, nobody could read or write. The great invention had not yet been made. Except for first-hand experience, almost everything we knew was passed on by word of mouth. As in the children's game "Whispers," over tens and hundreds of generations, information would slowly be distorted and lost.

Books changed all that. Books, purchasable at low cost, permit us to interrogate the past with high accuracy; to tap the wisdom of our species; to understand the point of view of others, and not just those in power; to contemplate — with the best teachers — the insights, painfully extracted from Nature, of the greatest minds that ever were, drawn from the entire planet and from all of our history. They allow people long dead to talk inside our heads. Books can accompany us everywhere. Books are patient where we are slow to understand, allow us to go over the hard parts as many times as we wish, and are never critical of our lapses...